What People Are Saying About NVC℠:

"Nonviolent Communication is a simple yet powerful methodology for communicating in a way that meets both parties' needs. This is one of the most useful books you will ever read."

—WILLIAM URY, co-author of *Getting to Yes* and author of *The Third Side*

"Marshall Rosenberg's book, *Nonviolent Communication: A Language of Life*, is essential reading for anyone who wants to improve their communication skills. Applying the concepts within the book will help guide the reader towards a more loving, compassionate, and non-violent way of understanding and functioning with others, and foster more compassion in the world. I highly recommend this book."

—MARIANNE WILLIAMSON, author of *Everyday Grace*, President Global Renaissance Alliance

"The extraordinary language of Nonviolent Communication is changing how parents relate to children, teachers to students, and how we all relate to each other and even to ourselves. It is precise, disciplined, and enormously compassionate. Most important, once we study NVC we can't ignore the potential for transformation that lies in any difficult relationship—if we only bother to communicate with skill and empathy."

—BERNIE GLASSMAN, President and Co-Founder Peacemaker Community

"Nonviolent Communication is a powerful tool for peace and partnership. It shows us how to listen empathically and also communicate our authentic feelings and needs. Marshall Rosenberg has a genius for developing and teaching practical skills urgently needed for a less violent, more caring world."

—RIANE EISLER, author of *The Chalice and The Blade*, *Tomorrow's Children*, and *The Power of Partnership*

"We learned to speak but not communicate and that has led to so much unnecessary personal and social misery. In this book you will find an amazingly effective language for saying what's on your mind and in your heart. Like so many essential and elegant systems, it's simple on the surface, challenging to use in the heat of the moment and powerful in its results."

—VICKI ROBIN, co-author of *Your Money or Your Life*

"Marshall Rosenberg provides us with the most effective tools to foster health and relationships. Nonviolent Communication connects soul to soul, creating a lot of healing. It is the missing element in what we do."

—DEEPAK CHOPRA, author of *Ageless Body, Timeless Mind*

"I believe the principles and techniques in this book can literally change the world, but more importantly, they can change the quality of your life with your spouse, your children, your neighbors, your co-workers and everyone else you interact with. I cannot recommend it highly enough."

—JACK CANFIELD, *Chicken Soup for the Soul* series

"Marshall Rosenberg's dynamic communication techniques transform potential conflicts into peaceful dialogues. You'll learn simple tools to defuse arguments and create compassionate connections with your family, friends, and other acquaintances. I highly recommend this book."

—JOHN GRAY, PH.D., author of *Men are From Mars, Women are from Venus*

"Rosenberg starts with the question: What happens to disconnect us from our compassion, leading us to behave violently and exploitively? Rosenberg makes some challenging points: that compliments and apologies operate in a system of oppression; that rewards are as harmful as punishment, that killing is the easy way out. His distinction between punitive and protective force—and how to discern when force is necessary—should be required reading for anyone making foreign policy or policing our streets. Demanding the ultimate form of responsibility—and vulnerability—it's no wonder that Rosenberg has received little media and mass attention. Well-written and laid out this book is accessible and easy to read."

—D. KILLIAN, On The Front Line, *Cleveland Free Times*

"Changing the way the world works sounds daunting, but Nonviolent Communication helps liberate us from ancient patterns of violence."
—FRANCIS LEFKOWITZ, *Body & Soul*

"Marshall's unique message gives teachers easy steps for peaceful communication and a new way to work with children and parents."
—BARBARA MOFFITT, Executive Director, National Center for Montessori Educators

"I appreciate how well Nonviolent Communication reduces a very complex and needful topic to utter simplicity."
—HAL DOIRON, Director, Columbine Community Citizen's Task Force

"*Nonviolent Communication* is a masterwork. Nationally, we talk peace. This book goes far beyond mere talk . . . it shows us how to TEACH peace."
—JAMES E. SHAW, PH.D., *Jack and Jill, Why They Kill*

"In our present age of uncivil discourse and mean-spirited demagoguery, racial hatreds and ethnic intolerance, the principles and practices outlined in *Nonviolent Communication* are as timely as they are necessary to the peaceful resolution of conflicts, personal or public, domestic or international."
—MIDWEST BOOK REVIEW, Taylor's Shelf

"*Nonviolent Communication* is filled with stories of mediations in many different situations: families, corporations, cops and gangs, Rwandan village tribal chiefs, Israelis and Palestinians. The author describes how, in numerous conflicts, once 'enemies' have been able to hear each other's needs, they are able to connect compassionately and find new solutions to previously 'impossible' impasses. He has compiled his ideas into an easy-to-read book that clearly explains this communication model. If you want to learn ways of more skillful speech, I highly recommend this book."
—DIANA LION, Buddhist Peace Fellowship, *Turning Wheel Magazine*

"I highly recommend Nonviolent Communication to anyone interested in creating more intimate relationships or exploring the connection between language and violence."

—KATE LIN, *The New Times*

"We have lived traumatic moments over and over again, moments of fear and panic, incomprehension, frustrations, disappointment, and injustice of all sorts, with no hope of escape. Those who have participated in Marshall Rosenberg's training have a real desire to use Nonviolent Communication as a peaceful alternative for ending this interminable Rwandan conflict."

—THEODORE NYILIDANDI, Rwandan Dept.
of Foreign Affairs - Kigali, Rwanda

"This book is essential reading for anyone seeking to end the unfulfilling cycles of argument in their relationships. Marshall Rosenberg offers a radical challenge to centuries of thought and language that create violence. If enough people actually learn Nonviolent Communication we may soon live in a more peaceful and compassionate world."

—WES TAYLOR, Progressive Health

"With the growth in today's dysfunctional families and the increase of violence in our schools, Nonviolent Communication is a godsend."

—LINDA C. STOEHR, Los Colinas Business News

"I had come to realize that my old communication style was very judgmental and full of faultfinding. Both my work associates and I were unhappy. My life is significantly changed due to practicing Nonviolent Communication. I am more settled and relaxed even when I am busy. I no longer feel the need to discover fault or place blame. Everyone is happy to be working with me for the first time in my 33 years of owning and operating my own businesses."

—A businessman in California

"If you care about healing the offender and the victims in the community, then it's paramount that beginnings be made. Nonviolent Communication is a very large step toward that goal."

—A prison inmate

"In addition to saving our marriage, Marshall's work is helping us to repair our relationships with our grown children and to relate more deeply with our parents and siblings. Marshall has shown a way to not only live, speak and act nonviolently, but a way to do so without sacrificing or compromising yourself or others. If angels do manifest in physical form here on this earth, then Marshall Rosenberg must be one."

—A reader in Arizona

"Nonviolent Communication has catalyzed a process of clarification/healing/empowerment in me that I could never have imagined. This process has impacted every area of my life and continues to unfold. For me, it unifies the spiritual truths I've found in all the world's religions. It facilitates and strengthens connections to others and its truths are experientially testable. In a workshop Marshall Rosenberg said that all the great religions have 'love' at their heart, and 'I'm just trying to figure out how to do that.' I stand in awe of the model this book teaches as a means of learning how to 'do' love and of its elegant simplicity."

—A reader in Florida

"Applying these principles to my life and using this easy four-step process has helped me change old conditioned beliefs and ways of acting. Nonviolent Communication allowed me to overcome my toxic conditioning and find the loving parent and person that was locked inside. Dr. Rosenberg has created a way to transform the violence in the world."

—A nurse in California

"As a professional in the field, I have read many books touting most of the topics covered in this book. But today I am ordering SEVERAL of these, particularly for the teenagers in my life. This book practices what it preaches, and I found the step-by-step approach, exercises, and examples to be clear and easy to practice."

—A reader in Maryland

I have never read a clearer, more straightforward, insightful book on communication. After studying and teaching assertiveness since the 70s, this book is a breath of fresh air. Rosenberg adds the brilliant insight into the linkage of feelings and needs and taking responsibility and creates a true tool. Amazingly easy to read, great examples, and challenging to put into practice—this book is a true gift to all of us.

—A reader in Washington

"The single toughest, most dangerous opponent I'd ever faced—the one that truly hurt me the most, causing me to spend 30 years of my life behind bars—was my own anger and fear. I write these words now, a gray haired old man, hoping to God—before you suffer what I've suffered—that it will cause you to listen and learn Nonviolent Communication. It will teach you how to recognize anger before it becomes violence, and how to understand, deal with, and take control of the rage you may feel."

—A prisoner writing to fellow inmates

"As a teacher, the process of Nonviolent Communication enables me to connect more deeply; children love and respond to that deep recognition. Parents remark that they feel heard. Solutions come more easily and naturally. Conflicts and misunderstandings with colleagues now become opportunities to create deeper connections. Anger, depression, shame and guilt become friends that help me wake to some vital need that is not being met. Read the book!"

—A teacher in Oregon

"My relationship with my husband, which was good already, has become even better. I have taught the method to many parents who have reported having gained a deeper understanding of their children, thus enhancing their relationship and decreasing tension and conflict."

—A reader in Illinois

Nonviolent
COMMUNICATION℠

A Language of Life

Marshall B. Rosenberg, Ph.D.

PuddleDancer
PRESS

P.O. Box 231129, Encinitas, CA 92023-1129
email@PuddleDancer.com • www.PuddleDancer.com

PuddleDancer Press, Permissions Dept.
P.O. Box 231129, Encinitas, CA 92023-1129
Fax: 1-858-759-6967, email@PuddleDancer.com

Nonviolent Communication: A Language of Life
2nd Edition Printing, August, 2003
        Author: Marshall B. Rosenberg, Ph.D.
        Editor: Lucy Leu
        Project Director: Jeanne Iler
        Cover and interior design: Lightbourne, www.lightbourne.com
        Cover photograph of Jerusalem artichoke: Eric Dresser

Manufactured in the United States of America

10 9 8 7 6 5

ISBN: 1-892005-03-4

                    Library of Congress Cataloging-in-Publication Data

        Rosenberg, Marshall B.
          Nonviolent communication : a language of life / by Marshall B.
        Rosenberg. -- 2nd ed.
              p. cm.
        Includes bibliographical references and index.
          ISBN: 1-892005-03-4
        1. Interpersonal communication.   2. Interpersonal relations. I.
        Title.
          BF637.C45R67 2003
          153.6--dc21
                                        2003010831

Contents

Acknowledgements

I'm grateful that I was able to study and work with Professor Carl Rogers at a time when he was researching the components of a helping relationship. The results of this research played a key role in the evolution of the process of communication that I will be describing in this book.

I will be forever grateful that Professor Michael Hakeem helped me to see the scientific limitations and the social and political dangers of practicing psychology in the way that I had been trained: a pathology-based understanding of human beings. Seeing the limitations of this model stimulated me to search for ways of practicing a different psychology, one based on a growing clarity about how we human beings were meant to live.

I'm grateful, too, for George Miller's and George Albee's efforts to alert psychologists to the need of finding better ways for "giving psychology away." They helped me see that the enormity of suffering on our planet requires more effective ways of distributing much-needed skills than can be offered by a clinical approach.

I would like to thank Lucy Leu for editing this book and creating the final manuscript; Rita Herzog and Kathy Smith for their editing assistance; and for the additional help of Darold Milligan, Sonia Nordenson, Melanie Sears, Bridget Belgrave, Marian Moore, Kittrell McCord, Virginia Hoyte, and Peter Weismiller.

Finally, I would like to express gratitude to my friend Annie Muller. Her encouragement to be clearer about the spiritual foundation of my work has strengthened that work and enriched my life.

Foreword

Arun Gandhi
Founder/President, M.K. Gandhi Institute for Nonviolence

Growing up as a person of color in apartheid South Africa in the 1940's was not something anyone relished. This was especially true if you were brutally reminded of your skin color every moment of every day. And then to be beaten up at the age of ten by white youths because they considered you too black, and then by black youths because they considered you too white, is a humiliating experience that could drive anyone to vengeful violence.

I was so outraged by my experiences that my parents decided to take me to India and leave me for some time with grandfather, the legendry M. K. Gandhi, so that I could learn from him how to deal with the anger, the frustration, the discrimination, and the humiliation that violent color prejudice can evoke in you. In those 18 months I learned more than I anticipated. My only regret now is that I was just 13 years old and a mediocre student at that. If only I was older, a bit wiser and a bit more thoughtful, I could have learned so much more. But one must be happy with what one has received and not be greedy—a fundamental lesson in nonviolent living. How can I forget this?

One of the many things I learned from grandfather is to understand the depth and breadth of nonviolence, and to acknowledge that we are all violent and that we need to bring about a qualitative change in our attitudes. We often don't acknowledge our violence because we are ignorant about it. We assume we are not violent because our vision of violence is one of fighting, killing, beating, and wars—the type of things that average individuals don't do.

To bring this home to me, grandfather made me draw a family tree of violence using the same principles as are used for a genealogical tree. His argument was that I would have a better appreciation of nonviolence if I understood and acknowledged the violence that exists in the world. He assisted me every evening to analyze the day's happenings—everything that I experienced, read about, saw or did to others—and put them down on the tree either under "physical" (if it was violence where physical force was used) or under "passive" (if it was the type of violence where the hurt was more emotional).

Within a few months I covered one wall in my room with acts of "passive" violence that grandfather described as being more insidious than "physical" violence. He then explained that passive violence ultimately generated anger in the victim who, as an individual or as a member of a collective, responded violently. In other words it is passive violence that fuels the fire of physical violence. It is because we don't understand or appreciate this concept that all our efforts to work for peace have either not fructified, or the peace that we achieved was only temporary. How can we extinguish a fire if we don't first cut off the fuel that ignites the inferno?

Grandfather always vociferously stressed the need for nonviolence in communications—something that Marshall Rosenberg has been doing admirably for many years through his writings and his seminars. I read with considerable interest Mr. Rosenberg's book, *Nonviolent Communication—A Language of Life*, and was impressed by the depth of his work and the simplicity of the solutions.

Unless, as grandfather would say, "we become the change we wish to see in the world," no change will ever take place. We are all, unfortunately, waiting for the other person to change first.

Nonviolence is not a strategy that can be used today and discarded tomorrow, nor is it something that makes you meek or a pushover. Nonviolence is about inculcating positive attitudes to replace the negative attitudes that dominate us. Everything that we do is conditioned by selfish motives—what's in it for me—and even more so in an overwhelmingly materialistic society that thrives on rugged individualism. None of these negative concepts is conducive to building a homogeneous family, community, society, or nation.

It is not important that we come together in a moment of crisis and show our patriotism by flying the flag; it is not enough that we become a superpower by building an arsenal that can destroy this earth several times over; it is not enough that we subjugate the rest of the world through our military might, because peace cannot be built on the foundations of fear.

Nonviolence means allowing the positive within you to emerge. Be dominated by love, respect, understanding, appreciation, compassion, and concern for others rather than the self-centered and selfish, greedy, hateful, prejudiced, suspicious, and aggressive attitudes that usually dominate our thinking. We often hear people say: "This world is ruthless and if you want to survive you must become ruthless, too." I humbly disagree with this contention.

This world is what we have made of it. If it is ruthless today it is because we have made it ruthless by our attitudes. If we change ourselves we can change the world, and changing ourselves begins with changing our language and methods of communication. I highly recommend reading this book, and applying the Nonviolent Communication process it teaches. It is a significant first step towards changing our communication and creating a compassionate world.

—Arun Gandhi

Words are Windows
(or They're Walls)

I feel so sentenced by your words,
I feel so judged and sent away,
Before I go I've got to know
Is that what you mean to say?
Before I rise to my defense,
Before I speak in hurt or fear,
Before I build that wall of words,
Tell me, did I really hear?
Words are windows, or they're walls,
They sentence us, or set us free.
When I speak and when I hear,
Let the love light shine through me.
There are things I need to say,
Things that mean so much to me,
If my words don't make me clear,
Will you help me to be free?
If I seemed to put you down,
If you felt I didn't care,
Try to listen through my words
To the feelings that we share.

—Ruth Bebermeyer

CHAPTER ONE

Giving from the Heart

The Heart of Nonviolent Communication

What I want in my life is compassion,
a flow between myself and others based
on a mutual giving from the heart.
—Marshall Rosenberg

Introduction

Believing that it is our nature to enjoy giving and receiving in a compassionate manner, I have been preoccupied most of my life with two questions. What happens to disconnect us from our compassionate nature, leading us to behave violently and exploitatively? And conversely, what allows some people to stay connected to their compassionate nature under even the most trying circumstances?

My preoccupation with these questions began in childhood, around the summer of 1943, when our family moved to Detroit, Michigan. The second week after we arrived, a race war erupted over an incident at a public park. More than forty people were killed in the next few days. Our neighborhood was situated in the center of the violence, and we spent three days locked in the house.

When the race riot ended and school began, I discovered that a name could be as dangerous as any skin color. When the teacher called my name during attendance, two boys glared at me and hissed, "Are you a kike?" I had never heard the word before and didn't know some people used it in a derogatory way to refer to Jews. After school, the two were waiting for me: they threw me to the ground, kicked and beat me.

Since that summer in 1943, I have been examining the two questions I mentioned. What empowers us, for example, to stay connected to our compassionate nature even under the worst circumstances? I am thinking of people like Etty Hillesum, who remained compassionate even while subjected to the grotesque conditions of a German concentration camp. As she wrote in her journal at the time,

> I am not easily frightened. Not because I am brave but because I know that I am dealing with human beings, and that I must try as hard as I can to understand everything that anyone ever does. And that was the real import of this morning: not that a disgruntled young Gestapo officer yelled at me, but that I felt no indignation, rather a real compassion, and would have liked to ask, 'Did you have a very unhappy childhood, has your girlfriend let you down?' Yes, he looked harassed and driven, sullen and weak. I should have liked to start treating him there and then, for I know that pitiful young men like that are dangerous as soon as they are let loose on mankind.
>
> —Etty Hillesum: A Diary.

While studying the factors that affect our ability to stay compassionate, I was struck by the crucial role of language and our use of words. I have since identified a specific approach to communicating—speaking and listening—that leads us to give from the heart, connecting us with ourselves and with each other in a way that allows our natural compassion to flourish. I call this approach Nonviolent Communication, using the term *nonviolence* as Gandhi used it—to refer to our natural state of compassion when violence has subsided from the heart. While we may not consider the way we talk to be "violent," our words often lead to hurt and pain, whether for others or ourselves. In some communities, the process I am describing is known as Compassionate Communication; the abbreviation "NVC" is used throughout this book to refer to Nonviolent or Compassionate Communication.

> NVC: a way of communicating that leads us to give from the heart.

A Way To Focus Attention

NVC is founded on language and communication skills that strengthen our ability to remain human, even under trying conditions. It contains nothing new; all that has been integrated into NVC has been known for centuries. The intent is to remind us about what we already know—about how we humans were meant to relate to one another—and to assist us in living in a way that concretely manifests this knowledge.

NVC guides us in reframing how we express ourselves and hear others. Instead of being habitual, automatic reactions, our words become conscious responses based firmly on an awareness of what we are perceiving, feeling, and wanting. We are led to express ourselves with honesty and clarity, while simultaneously paying others a respectful and empathic attention. In any exchange, we come to hear our own deeper needs and those of others. NVC trains us to observe carefully, and to be able to specify behaviors and conditions that are affecting us. We learn to identify and clearly articulate what we are concretely wanting in a given situation. The form is simple, yet powerfully transformative.

As NVC replaces our old patterns of defending, withdrawing, or attacking in the face of judgment and criticism, we come to perceive ourselves and others, as well as our intentions and relationships, in a new light. Resistance, defensiveness, and violent reactions are minimized. When we focus on clarifying what is being observed,

> We perceive relationships in a new light when we use NVC to hear our own deeper needs and those of others.

felt, and needed rather than on diagnosing and judging, we discover the depth of our own compassion. Through its emphasis on deep listening—to ourselves as well as others—NVC fosters respect, attentiveness, and empathy, and engenders a mutual desire to give from the heart.

Although I refer to it as "a process of communication" or a "language of compassion," NVC is more than a process or a language. On a deeper level, it is an ongoing reminder to keep our attention focused on a place where we are more likely to get what we are seeking.

There is a story of a man under a street lamp searching for something on all fours. A policeman passing by asked what he was doing. "Looking for my car keys," replied the man, who appeared slightly drunk. "Did you drop them here?" inquired the officer. "No," answered the man, "I dropped them in the alley." Seeing the policeman's baffled expression, the man hastened to explain, "But the light is much better here."

I find that my cultural conditioning leads me to focus attention on places where I am unlikely to get what I want. I developed NVC as a way to train my attention—to shine the light of consciousness—on places that have the potential to yield what I am seeking. What I want in my life is compassion, a flow between myself and others based on a mutual giving from the heart.

> Let's shine the light of consciousness on places where we can hope to find what we are seeking.

This quality of compassion, which I refer to as "giving from the heart," is expressed in the following lyrics by my friend, Ruth Bebermeyer:

I never feel more given to
than when you take from me —
when you understand the joy I feel
   giving to you.
And you know my giving isn't done
   to put you in my debt,
but because I want to live the love
   I feel for you.
To receive with grace
may be the greatest giving.
There's no way I can separate
   the two.
When you give to me,
I give you my receiving.
When you take from me, I feel so
   given to.

  —Song "Given To" (1978) by Ruth Bebermeyer
  from the album, Given To.

When we give from the heart, we do so out of a joy that springs forth whenever we willingly enrich another person's life. This kind of giving benefits both the giver and the receiver. The receiver enjoys the gift without worrying about the consequences that accompany gifts given out of fear, guilt, shame, or desire for gain. The giver benefits from the enhanced self-esteem that results when we see our efforts contributing to someone's well-being.

The use of NVC does not require that the persons with whom we are communicating be literate in NVC or even motivated to relate to us compassionately. If we stay with the principles of NVC, motivated solely to give and receive compassionately, and do everything we can to let others know this is our only motive, they will join us in the process and eventually we will be able to respond compassionately to one another. I'm not saying that this always happens quickly. I do maintain, however, that compassion inevitably blossoms when we stay true to the principles and process of NVC.

The NVC Process

To arrive at a mutual desire to give from the heart, we focus the light of consciousness on four areas—referred to as the four components of the NVC model.

First, we observe what is actually happening in a situation: what are we observing others saying or doing that is either enriching or not enriching our life? The trick is to be able to articulate this observation without introducing any judgment or evaluation—to simply say what people are doing that we either like or don't like. Next, we state how we feel when we observe this action: are we hurt, scared, joyful, amused, irritated, etc.? And thirdly, we say what needs of ours are connected to the feelings we have identified. An awareness of these three components is present when we use NVC to clearly and honestly express how we are.

Four components of NVC:
1. observation
2. feeling
3. needs
4. request

For example, a mother might express these three pieces to her teenage son by saying, "Felix, when I see two balls of soiled socks under the coffee table and another three next to the TV, I feel irritated because I am needing more order in the rooms that we share in common."

She would follow immediately with the fourth component—a very specific request: "Would you be willing to put your socks in your room or in the washing machine?" This fourth component addresses what we are wanting from the other person that would enrich our lives or make life more wonderful for us.

Thus, part of NVC is to express these four pieces of information very clearly, whether verbally or by other means. The other aspect of this communication consists of receiving the same four pieces of information from others. We connect with them by first sensing what they are observing, feeling, and needing, and then discover what would enrich their lives by receiving the fourth piece, their request.

As we keep our attention focused on the areas mentioned, and help others do likewise, we establish a flow of communication, back and forth, until compassion manifests naturally: what I am observing, feeling, and needing; what I am requesting to enrich my life; what you are observing, feeling, and needing; what you are requesting to enrich your life. . . .

NVC Process

The concrete actions we are
observing that are affecting our well-being

How we *feel* in relation
to what we are observing

The *needs*, values, desires, etc.
that are creating our feelings

The concrete actions we *request*
in order to enrich our lives

When we use this process, we may begin either by expressing ourselves or by empathically receiving these four pieces of information from others. Although we will learn to listen for and verbally express each of these components in Chapters 3–6, it is important to keep in mind that NVC does not consist of a set formula, but adapts to various situations as well as personal and cultural styles. While I conveniently refer to NVC as a "process" or "language," it is possible to experience all four pieces of the process without uttering a single

Two parts of NVC:
1. expressing honesty through the four components
2. receiving empathically through the four components

word. The essence of NVC is to be found in our consciousness of these four components, not in the actual words that are exchanged.

Applying NVC In Our Lives And World

When we use NVC in our interactions—with ourselves, with another person, or in a group—we become grounded in our natural state of compassion. It is therefore an approach that can be effectively applied at all levels of communication and in diverse situations:

  intimate relationships
  families
  schools
  organizations and institutions
  therapy and counseling
  diplomatic and business negotiations
  disputes and conflicts of any nature

Some people use NVC to create greater depth and caring in their intimate relationships:

> When I learned how I can receive (hear), as well as give (express), through using NVC, I went beyond feeling attacked and 'door mattish' to really listening to words and extracting their underlying feelings. I discovered a very hurting man to whom I had been married for 28 years. He had asked me for a divorce the weekend before the [NVC] workshop. To make a long story short, we are here today—together, and I appreciate the contribution [it has] made to our happy ending. . . . I learned to listen for feelings, to express my needs, to accept answers that I didn't always want to hear. He is not here to make me happy, nor am I here to create happiness for him. We have both learned to grow, to accept and to love, so that we can each be fulfilled.
>
> —workshop participant in San Diego

Others use it to build more effective relationships at work. A teacher writes:

> I have been using NVC in my special education classroom for about one year. It can work even with children who have language delays, learning difficulties, and behavior problems. One student in our classroom spits, swears, screams, and stabs other students with pencils when they get near his desk. I cue him with, 'Please say that another way. Use your giraffe talk.' [Giraffe puppets are used in some workshops as a teaching aid to demonstrate NVC.] He immediately stands up straight, looks at the person towards whom his anger is directed, and says calmly, 'Would you please move away from my desk? I feel angry when you stand so close to me.' The other students might respond with something like 'Sorry! I forgot it bothers you.'
>
> I began to think about my frustration with this child and to try to discover what I needed from him (besides harmony and order). I realized how much time I had put into lesson planning and how my need for creativity and contribution were being short-circuited in order to manage behavior. Also, I felt I was not meeting the educational needs of the other students. When he was acting out in class, I began to say, 'I need you to share my attention.' It might take a hundred cues a day, but he got the message and would usually get involved in the lesson.
>
> —teacher, Chicago, Illinois

A doctor writes:

> I use NVC more and more in my medical practice. Some patients ask me whether I am a psychologist, saying that usually their doctors are not interested in the way they live their lives or deal with their diseases. NVC helps me understand what the patients' needs are and what they need to hear at a given moment. I find this particularly helpful in relating to patients with hemophilia and AIDS because there is so much anger and pain that the patient/healthcare-provider relationship is often seriously impaired. Recently a woman with AIDS, whom I have been treating for the past five years, told me that what has helped her the most have been my attempts to find ways for her to enjoy her daily life. My use of NVC helps me a lot in this respect. Often in the past, when I knew that a patient had a fatal disease, I myself would get caught in the prognosis, and it was hard for me to sincerely encourage them to live their lives. With NVC, I have developed a new consciousness as well as a new language. I am amazed to see how much it fits in with my medical practice. I feel more energy and joy in my work as I become increasingly engaged in the dance of NVC.
>
> —physician in Paris

Still others use this process in the political arena. A French cabinet member visiting her sister remarked how differently the sister and her husband were communicating and responding to each other. Encouraged by their descriptions of NVC, she mentioned that she was scheduled the following week to negotiate some sensitive issues between France and Algeria regarding adoption procedures. Though time was limited, we dispatched a French-speaking trainer to Paris to work with the cabinet minister. She later attributed much of the success of her negotiations in Algeria to her newly acquired communication techniques.

In Jerusalem, during a workshop attended by Israelis of varying political persuasions, participants used NVC to express themselves regarding the highly contested issue of the West Bank. Many of the Israeli settlers who have established themselves on the West Bank believe that they are fulfilling a religious mandate by doing so, and they are locked in conflict not only with Palestinians but also with other Israelis who recognize the Palestinian hope for national sovereignty in this region. During a session, one of my trainers and I modeled empathic hearing through NVC, and then invited participants to take turns role-playing each other's position. After twenty minutes, a settler announced her willingness to consider relinquishing her land claims and moving out of the West Bank into internationally recognized Israeli territory if her political opponents were able to listen to her in the way she had just been listened to.

Worldwide, NVC now serves as a valuable resource for communities facing violent conflicts and severe ethnic, religious, or political tensions. The spread of NVC training and its use in mediation by people in conflict in Israel, the Palestinian Authority, Nigeria, Rwanda, Sierra Leone, and elsewhere have been a source of particular gratification for me. My associates and I were once in Belgrade over three highly charged days training citizens working for peace. When we first arrived, expressions of despair were visibly etched on the trainees' faces, for their country was then enmeshed in a brutal war in Bosnia and Croatia. As the training progressed, we heard the ring of laughter in their voices as they shared their profound gratitude and joy for having found the empowerment they were seeking. Over the next two weeks, during trainings in Croatia, Israel, and Palestine, we again saw desperate citizens in war-torn countries regaining their spirits and confidence from the NVC training they received.

I feel blessed to be able to travel throughout the world teaching people a process of communication that gives them power and joy. Now, with this book, I am pleased and excited to be able to share the richness of Nonviolent Communication with you.

Summary

NVC helps us connect with each other and ourselves in a way that allows our natural compassion to flourish. It guides us to reframe the way we express ourselves and listen to others by focusing our consciousness on four areas: what we are observing, feeling, and needing and what we are requesting to enrich our lives. NVC fosters deep listening, respect, and empathy and engenders a mutual desire to give from the heart. Some people use NVC to respond compassionately to themselves, some to create greater depth in their personal relationships, and still others to build effective relationships at work or in the political arena. Worldwide, NVC is used to mediate disputes and conflicts at all levels.

NVC in Action

"Murderer, Assassin, Child Killer!"

Interspersed throughout the book are dialogues entitled NVC in Action. These dialogues intend to impart the flavor of an actual exchange where a speaker is applying the principles of Nonviolent Communication. However, NVC is not simply a language or a set of techniques for using words; the consciousness and intent that it embraces may be expressed through silence, a quality of presence, as well as through facial expressions and body language. The NVC in Action dialogues you will be reading are necessarily distilled and abridged versions of real-life exchanges, where moments of silent empathy, stories, humor, gestures, etc. would all contribute to a more natural flow of connection between the two parties than might be apparent when dialogues are condensed in print.

I was presenting Nonviolent Communication in a mosque at Deheisha Refugee Camp in Bethlehem to about 170 Palestinian Moslem men. Attitudes toward Americans at that time were not favorable. As I was speaking, I suddenly noticed a wave of muffled commotion fluttering through the audience. "They're whispering that you are American!" my translator alerted me, just as a gentleman in the audience leapt to his feet. Facing me squarely, he hollered at the top of his lungs, "Murderer!" Immediately a dozen other voices joined him in chorus: "Assassin!" "Child-killer!" "Murderer!"

Fortunately, I was able to focus my attention on what the man was feeling and needing. In this case, I had some cues. On the way into the refugee camp, I had seen several empty tear gas canisters that had been shot into the camp the night before. Clearly marked on each canister were the words "Made in U.S.A." I knew that the refugees harbored a lot of anger toward the U.S. for supplying tear gas and other weapons to Israel.

I addressed the man who had called me a murderer:

I: Are you angry because you would like my government to use its resources differently? *(I didn't know whether my guess was correct, but what is critical is my sincere effort to connect with his feeling and need.)*

He: Damn right I'm angry! You think we need tear gas? We need sewers, not your tear gas! We need housing! We need to have our own country!

I: So you're furious and would appreciate some support in improving your living conditions and gaining political independence?

He: Do you know what it's like to live here for twenty-seven years the way I have with my family—children and all? Have you got the faintest idea what that's been like for us?

I: Sounds like you're feeling very desperate and you're wondering whether I or anybody else can really understand what it's like to be living under these conditions. Am I hearing you right?

He: You want to understand? Tell me, do you have children? Do they go to school? Do they have playgrounds? My son is sick! He plays in open sewage! His classroom has no books! Have you seen a school that has no books?

I: I hear how painful it is for you to raise your children here; you'd like me to know that what you want is what all parents want for their children—a good education, opportunity to play and grow in a healthy environment . . .

He: That's right, the basics! Human rights—isn't that what you Americans call it? Why don't more of you come here and see what kind of human rights you're bringing here!

I: You'd like more Americans to be aware of the enormity of the suffering here and to look more deeply at the consequences of our political actions?

Our dialogue continued, with him expressing his pain for nearly twenty more minutes, and I listening for the feeling and need behind each statement. I didn't agree or disagree. I received his words, not as attacks, but as gifts from a fellow human willing to share his soul and deep vulnerabilities with me.

Once the gentleman felt understood, he was able to hear me as I explained my purpose for being at the camp. An hour later, the same man who had called me a murderer was inviting me to his home for a Ramadan dinner.

CHAPTER TWO

Communication That Blocks Compassion

Do not judge, and you will not be judged.
For as you judge others, so you will yourselves be judged . . .
—Holy Bible, Matthew 7:1

In studying the question of what alienates us from our natural state of compassion, I have identified specific forms of language and communication that I believe contribute to our behaving violently toward each other and ourselves.

> Certain ways of communicating alienate us from our natural state of compassion

I use the term "life-alienating communication" to refer to these forms of communication.

Moralistic Judgments

One kind of life-alienating communication is the use of moralistic judgments that imply wrongness or badness on the part of people who don't act in harmony with our values. Such judgments are reflected in language such as, "The problem with you is that you're too selfish." "She's lazy." "They're prejudiced." "It's inappropriate." Blame, insults, put-downs, labels, criticism, comparisons, and diagnoses are all forms of judgment.

> In the world of judgments, our concern centers on WHO "IS" WHAT.

The Sufi poet Rumi once wrote, "Out beyond ideas of wrongdoing and right-doing, there is a field. I'll meet you there." Life-alienating communication, however, traps us in a world of ideas about rightness and wrongness—a world of judgments; it is a language rich with words that classify and dichotomize people and their actions. When we speak this language, we judge others and their behavior while preoccupying ourselves with who's good, bad, normal, abnormal, responsible, irresponsible, smart, ignorant, etc.

Long before I reached adulthood, I learned to communicate in an impersonal way that did not require me to reveal what was going on inside of myself. When I encountered people or behaviors I either didn't like or didn't understand, I would react in terms of their wrongness. If my teachers assigned a task I didn't want to do, they were "mean" or "unreasonable." If someone pulled out in front of me in traffic, my reaction would be, "You idiot!" When we speak this language, we think and communicate in terms of what's wrong with others for behaving in certain ways, or occasionally, what's wrong with ourselves for not understanding or responding as we would like. Our attention is focused on classifying, analyzing, and determining levels of wrongness rather than on what we and others need and are not getting. Thus if my partner wants more affection than I'm giving her, she is "needy and dependent." But if I want more affection than she is giving me, then she is "aloof and insensitive." If my colleague is more concerned about details than I am, he is "picky and compulsive." On the other hand, if I am more concerned about details than he is, he is "sloppy and disorganized."

> Analyses of others are actually expressions of our own needs and values.

It is my belief that all such analyses of other human beings are tragic expressions of our own values and needs. They are tragic because, when we express our values and needs in this form, we increase defensiveness and resistance to them among the very people whose behaviors are of concern to us. Or, if they do agree to act in harmony with our values because they concur with our analysis of their wrongness, they will likely do so out of fear, guilt, or shame.

We all pay dearly when people respond to our values and needs, not out of a desire to give from the heart, but out of fear, guilt, or shame. Sooner or later, we will experience the consequences of diminished goodwill on the part of those who comply with our values out of a sense of either external or internal coercion. They, too, pay emotionally, for they are likely to feel resentment and decreased self-esteem when they respond to us out of fear, guilt, or shame. Furthermore, each time others associate us in their minds with any of those feelings, we decrease the likelihood of their responding compassionately to our needs and values in the future.

It is important here not to confuse *value judgments* and *moralistic judgments*. All of us make value judgments as to the qualities we value in life; for example, we might value honesty, freedom, or peace. Value judgments reflect our beliefs of how life can best be served. We make *moralistic judgments* of people and behaviors that fail to support our value judgments, e.g. "Violence is bad. People who kill others are evil." Had we been raised speaking a language that facilitated the expression of compassion, we would have learned to articulate our needs and values directly, rather than to insinuate wrongness when they have not been met. For example, instead of "Violence is bad," we might say instead, "I am fearful of the use of violence to resolve conflicts; I value the resolution of human conflicts through other means."

The relationship between language and violence is the subject of psychology professor O.J. Harvey's research at the University of Colorado. He took random samples of pieces of literature from many countries over the world and tabulated the frequency of words that classify and judge people. His study shows a high correlation between the frequent use of such words and incidences of violence. It does not surprise me to hear that there is considerably less violence in cultures where people think in terms of human needs than in cultures where people label one another as "good" or "bad" and believe that the "bad" ones deserve to be punished. In 75 percent of the television programs shown during hours when

American children are most likely to be watching, the hero either kills people or beats them up. This violence typically constitutes the "climax" of the show.

> Classifying and judging people promote violence.

Viewers, having been taught that bad guys deserve to be punished, take pleasure in watching this violence.

At the root of much, if not all, violence—whether verbal, psychological, or physical, whether among family members, tribes, or nations—is a kind of thinking that attributes the cause of conflict to wrongness in one's adversaries, and a corresponding inability to think of oneself or others in terms of vulnerability—what one might be feeling, fearing, yearning for, missing, etc. We saw this dangerous way of thinking during the Cold War. Our leaders viewed Russians as an "evil empire" bent on destroying the American way of life. Russian leaders referred to the people of the United States as "imperialist oppressors" who were trying to subjugate them. Neither side acknowledged the fear lurking behind such labels.

Making Comparisons

Another form of judgment is the use of comparisons. In his book, *How to Make Yourself Miserable*, Dan Greenberg demonstrates through humor the insidious power that comparative thinking can exert over us. He suggests that if readers have a sincere desire to make life miserable for themselves, they might learn to compare themselves to other people. For those unfamiliar with this practice, he provides a few exercises. The first one displays full-length pictures of a man and a woman who embody ideal physical beauty by contemporary media standards. Readers are instructed to take their own body measurements, compare them to those superimposed on the pictures of the attractive specimens, and dwell on the differences.

> Comparisons are a form of judgment.

This exercise produces what it promises: we start to feel miserable as we engage in these comparisons. By the time we're as depressed as we think possible, we turn the page to discover that the first exercise was a mere warm-up. Since physical beauty is relatively superficial, Greenberg now provides an opportunity to compare ourselves on something that matters: achievement. He resorts to the phone book to give readers a few random individuals to compare them-selves with. The first name he claims to have pulled out of the phone book is Wolfgang Amadeus Mozart. Greenberg lists the languages Mozart spoke and the major pieces he had composed by the time he was a teenager. The exercise then instructs readers to recall their own achievements at their current stage of life, to compare them with what Mozart had accomplished by age twelve, and to dwell on the differences.

Even readers who never emerge from the self-induced misery of this exercise might see how powerfully this type of thinking blocks compassion, both for oneself and for others.

Denial Of Responsibility

Another kind of life-alienating communication is the denial of responsibility. Life-alienating communication clouds our awareness that we are each responsible for our own thoughts, feelings, and actions. The use of the common expression "have to" as in "There are some things you have to do, whether you like it or not" illustrates how

> Our language obscures awareness of personal responsibility.

personal responsibility for our actions is obscured in such speech. The phrase "makes one feel" as in "You make me feel guilty" is another example of how language facilitates the denial of personal responsibility for our own feelings and thoughts.

In her book, *Eichmann in Jerusalem*, which documents the war crimes trial of Nazi officer Adolph Eichmann, Hannah Arendt quotes Eichmann saying that he and his fellow officers had their own name for the responsibility-denying language they used. They called it "Amtssprache," loosely translated into English as "office talk" or "bureaucratese." For example, if asked why they took a certain action, the response might be, "I had to." If asked why they "had to," the answer would be, "Superiors' orders."

"Company policy." "It was the law."

We deny responsibility for our actions when we attribute their cause to:

- Vague, impersonal forces
  "I cleaned my room because I had to."
- Our condition, diagnosis, personal or psychological history
  "I drink because I am an alcoholic."
- The actions of others
  "I hit my child because he ran into the street."
- The dictates of authority
  "I lied to the client because the boss told me to."
- Group pressure
  "I started smoking because all my friends did."
- Institutional policies, rules, and regulations
  "I have to suspend you for this infraction because it's the school policy."
- Gender roles, social roles, or age roles
  "I hate going to work, but I do it because I am a husband and a father."
- Uncontrollable impulses
  "I was overcome by my urge to eat the candy bar."

Once, during a discussion among parents and teachers on the dangers of a language that implies absence of choice, a woman objected angrily, "But there are some things you have to do whether you like it or not! And I see nothing wrong with telling my children that there are things they have to do too." Asked for an example of something she "had to do," she retorted, "That's easy! When I leave here tonight, I have to go home and cook. I hate cooking! I hate it with a passion, but I have been doing it every day for twenty years, even when I've been as sick as a dog, because it's one of those things you just have to do." I told her I was sad to hear her spending so much of her life doing something she hated because she felt compelled to, and hoped that she might find happier possibilities by learning the language of NVC.

I am pleased to report that she was a rapid student. At the end of the workshop, she actually went home and announced to her family that she no longer wanted to cook. The opportunity for some feedback from her family came three weeks later when her two sons arrived at a workshop. I was curious to know how they had reacted to their mother's announcement. The elder son sighed, "Marshall, I just said to myself, 'Thank God!'" Seeing my puzzled look, he explained, "I thought to myself, maybe finally she won't be complaining at every meal!"

> We can replace language that implies lack of choice with language that acknowledges choice.

Another time, when I was consulting for a school district, a teacher remarked, "I hate giving grades. I don't think they are helpful and they create a lot of anxiety on the part of students. But I have to give grades: it's the district policy." We had just been practicing how to introduce language in the classroom that heightens consciousness of responsibility for one's actions. I suggested that the teacher translate the statement "I have to give grades because it's district policy" to "I choose to give grades because I want . . . " She answered without hesitation, "I choose to give grades because I want to keep my job," while hastening to add, "But I don't like saying it that way. It makes me feel so responsible for what I'm doing." "That's why I want you to do it that way," I replied.

> We are dangerous when we are not conscious of our responsibility for how we behave, think, and feel.

I share the sentiments of French novelist and journalist George Bernanos when he says,

> **I** have thought for a long time now that if, some day, the increasing efficiency for the technique of destruction finally causes our species to disappear from the earth, it will not be cruelty that will be responsible for our extinction and still less, of course, the indignation that cruelty awakens and the reprisals and

vengeance that it brings upon itself . . . but the docility, the lack of responsibility of the modern man, his base subservient acceptance of every common decree. The horrors that we have seen, the still greater horrors we shall presently see, are not signs that rebels, insubordinate, untamable men are increasing in number throughout the world, but rather that there is a constant increase in the number of obedient, docile men. *,,*

Other Forms Of Life-Alienating Communication

Communicating our desires as demands is another form of language that blocks compassion. A demand explicitly or implicitly threatens listeners with blame or punishment if they fail to comply. It is a common form of communication in our culture, especially among those who hold positions of authority.

My children gave me some invaluable lessons about demands. Somehow I had gotten it into my head that, as a parent, my job was to make demands. I learned, however, that I could make all the demands in the world but still couldn't make the children do anything.

We can never make people do anything.

This is a humbling lesson in power for those of us who believe that, because we're a parent, teacher, or manager, our job is to change other people and make them behave. Here were these youngsters letting me know that I couldn't make them do anything. All I could do was make them wish they had—through punishment. Then eventually they taught me that any time I was foolish enough to make them wish they had complied by punishing them, they had ways of making me wish that I hadn't!

We will examine this subject again when we learn to differentiate requests from demands—an important part of NVC.

Thinking based on "who deserves what" blocks compassionate communication.

Life-alienating communication is also associated with the concept that certain actions merit reward while others merit punishment. This thinking is expressed by the word "deserve" as in

"He deserves to be punished for what he did." It assumes "badness" on the part of people who behave in certain ways, and calls for punishment to make them repent and change their behavior. I believe it is in everyone's interest that people change, not in order to avoid punishment, but because they see the change as benefiting themselves.

Most of us grew up speaking a language that encourages us to label, compare, demand, and pronounce judgments rather than to be aware of what we are feeling and needing. I believe life-alienating communication is rooted in views of human nature that have exerted their influence for several centuries. These views stress our innate evil and deficiency, and a need for education to control our inherently undesirable nature. Such education often leaves us questioning whether there is something wrong with whatever feelings and needs we may be experiencing. We learn early to cut ourselves off from what's going on within ourselves.

> Life-alienating communication has deep philosophical and political roots.

Life-alienating communication both stems from and supports hierarchical or domination societies. Where large populations are controlled by a small number of individuals for their own benefit, it would be to the interest of kings, czars, nobles, etc. that the masses be educated in a way that renders them slave-like in mentality. The language of wrongness, "should" and "have to" is perfectly suited for this purpose: the more people are trained to think in terms of moralistic judgments that imply wrongness and badness, the more they are being trained to look outside themselves—to outside authorities—for the definition of what constitutes right, wrong, good and bad. When we are in contact with our feelings and needs, we humans no longer make good slaves and underlings.

Summary

It is our nature to enjoy giving and receiving compassionately. We have, however, learned many forms of "life-alienating communication" that lead us to speak and behave in ways that injure others and ourselves. One form of life-alienating communication is the use of moralistic judgments that imply wrongness or badness on the part of those who don't act in harmony with our values. Another form of such communication is the use of comparisons, which can block compassion both for others and ourselves. Life-alienating communication also obscures our awareness that we are each responsible for our own thoughts, feelings, and actions. Communicating our desires in the form of demands is yet another characteristic of language that blocks compassion.

CHAPTER THREE

Observing Without Evaluating

> *"OBSERVE!! There are few things as*
> *important, as religious, as that."*
> —Frederick Buechner, minister

I can handle your telling me
what I did or didn't do.
And I can handle your interpretations
but please don't mix the two.

If you want to confuse any issue,
I can tell you how to do it:
Mix together what I do
with how you react to it.

Tell me that you're disappointed
with the unfinished chores you see,
But calling me "irresponsible"
is no way to motivate me.

And tell me that you're feeling hurt
when I say "no" to your advances,
But calling me a frigid man
won't increase your future chances.

Yes, I can handle your telling me
what I did or didn't do,
And I can handle your interpretations,
but please don't mix the two.

—Marshall Rosenberg

The first component of NVC entails the *separation* of observation from evaluation. We need to clearly observe what we are seeing, hearing, or touching that is affecting our sense of well-being, without mixing in any evaluation.

Observations are an important element in NVC, where we wish to clearly and honestly express how we are to another person. When we combine observation with evaluation, however, we decrease the likelihood that others will hear our intended message. Instead, they are apt to hear criticism and thus resist what we are saying.

NVC does not mandate that we remain completely objective and refrain from evaluating. It only requires that we maintain a separation between our observations and our evaluations. NVC is a process language that discourages static generalizations; instead, evaluations are to be based on observations *specific to time and context.* Semanticist Wendell Johnson pointed out that we create many problems for ourselves by using static language to express or capture a reality that is ever changing: "Our language is an imperfect instrument created by ancient and ignorant men. It is an animistic language that invites us to talk about stability and constants, about similarities and normal and kinds, about magical transformations, quick cures, simple problems, and final solutions. Yet the world we try to symbolize with this language is a world of process, change, differences, dimensions, functions, relationships, growths, interactions, developing, learning, coping, complexity. And the mismatch of our ever-changing world and our relatively static language forms is part of our problem."

> When we combine observation with evaluation, people are apt to hear criticism.

A colleague of mine, Ruth Bebermeyer, contrasts static and process language in a song that illustrates the difference between evaluation and observation.

I've never seen a lazy man;
I've seen a man who never ran
while I watched him, and I've seen
a man who sometimes slept between
lunch and dinner, and who'd stay
at home upon a rainy day,
but he was not a lazy man.
Before you call me crazy,
think, was he a lazy man or
did he just do things we label "lazy"?

I've never seen a stupid kid;
I've seen a kid who sometimes did
things I didn't understand
or things in ways I hadn't planned;
I've seen a kid who hadn't seen
the same places where I had been,
but he was not a stupid kid.
Before you call him stupid,
think, was he a stupid kid or did he
just know different things than you did?

I've looked as hard as I can look
but never ever seen a cook;
I saw a person who combined
ingredients on which we dined,
A person who turned on the heat
and watched the stove that cooked the meat—
I saw those things but not a cook.
Tell me, when you're looking,
Is it a cook you see or is it someone
doing things that we call cooking?

What some of us call lazy
some call tired or easy-going,

what some of us call stupid
some just call a different knowing,
so I've come to the conclusion,
it will save us all confusion
if we don't mix up what we can see
with what is our opinion.
Because you may, I want to say also;
I know that's only my opinion.

While the effects of negative labels such as "lazy" and "stupid" may be more obvious, even a positive or an apparently neutral label such as "cook" limits our perception of the totality of another person's being.

The Highest Form Of Human Intelligence

The Indian philosopher J. Krishnamurti once remarked that observing without evaluating is the highest form of human intelligence. When I first read this statement, the thought, "What nonsense!" shot through my mind before I realized that I had just made an evaluation. For most of us, it is difficult to make observations of people and their behavior that are free of judgment, criticism, or other forms of analysis.

I became acutely aware of this difficulty while working with an elementary school where the staff and principal often reported communication difficulties. The district superintendent had requested that I help them resolve the conflict. First I was to confer with the staff, and then with the staff and principal together.

I opened the meeting by asking the staff, "What is the principal doing that conflicts with your needs?" "He has a big mouth!" came the swift response. My question called for an observation, but while "big mouth" gave me information on how this teacher evaluated the principal, it failed to describe what the principal *said or did* that led to the teacher's interpretation that he had a "big mouth."

When I pointed this out, a second teacher offered, "I know what he means: the principal talks too much!" Instead of a clear observation of the principal's behavior, this was also an evaluation—of how much the principal talked. A third teacher then declared, "He thinks only he has anything worth saying." I explained that inferring what another person is thinking is not the same as observing his behavior. Finally a fourth teacher ventured, "He wants to be the center of attention all the time." After I remarked that this too was an inference—of what another person is wanting—two teachers blurted in unison, "Well, your question is very hard to answer!"

We subsequently worked together to create a list identifying *specific behaviors* on the part of the principal that bothered them, and made sure that the list was free of evaluation. For example, the principal told stories about his childhood and war experiences during faculty meetings, with the result that meetings sometimes ran 20 minutes overtime. When I asked whether they had ever communicated their annoyance to the principal, the staff replied they had tried, but only through evaluative comments. They had never made reference to specific behaviors—such as his story telling—and agreed to bring these up when we were all to meet together.

Almost as soon as the meeting began, I saw what the staff had been telling me. No matter what was being discussed, the principal would interject, "This reminds me of the time . . . " and then launch into a story about his childhood or war experience. I waited for the staff to voice their discomfort around the principal's behavior. However, instead of Nonviolent Communication, they applied nonverbal condemnation. Some rolled their eyes; other yawned pointedly; one stared at his watch.

I endured this painful scenario until finally I asked, "Isn't anyone going to say something?" An awkward silence ensued. The teacher who had spoken first at our meeting screwed up his courage, looked directly at the principal, and said, "Ed, you have a big mouth."

As this story illustrates, it's not always easy to shed our old habits and master the ability to separate observation from evaluation. Eventually, the teachers succeeded in clarifying for the principal the specific actions that led to their concern. The principal listened earnestly and then pressed, "Why didn't one of you tell me before?" He admitted he was aware of his story-telling habit, and then began a story pertaining to this habit! I interrupted him, observing (good-naturedly) that he was doing it again. We ended our meeting developing ways for the staff to let their principal know, in a gentle way, when his stories weren't appreciated.

Distinguishing Observations From Evaluations

The following table distinguishes observations that are separate from evaluation from those that have evaluation mixed in.

Communication	Example of observation with evaluation mixed in	Example of observation separate from evaluation
1. Use of verb *to be* without indication that the evaluator accepts responsibility for the evaluation	You are too generous.	When I see you give all your lunch money to others I think you being too generous.
2. Use of verbs with evaluative connotations	Doug procrastinates.	Doug only studies for exams the night before.
3. Implication that one's inferences about another person's thoughts, feelings, intentions, or desires are the only ones possible	She won't get her work in.	I don't think she'll get her work in. *or* She said, "I won't get my work in."
4. Confusion of prediction with certainty	If you don't eat balanced meals, your health will be impaired.	If you don't eat balanced meals, I fear that your health may be impaired.
5. Failure to be specific about referents	Minorities don't take care of their property.	I have not seen the minority family living at 1679 Ross shovel the snow on their sidewalk.

6. Use of words denoting ability without indicating that an evaluation is being made	Hank Smith is a poor soccer player.	Hank Smith has not scored a goal in 20 games.
7. Use of adverb and adjectives in ways that do not signify an evaluation has been made	Jim is ugly.	Jim's looks don't appeal to me.

Note: The words *always, never, ever, whenever,* etc. express observations when used in the following ways:

- Whenever I have observed Jack on the phone, he has spoken for at least 30 minutes.
- I cannot recall your ever writing to me.

Sometimes such words are used as exaggerations, in which case observations and evaluations are being mixed:

- You are always busy.
- She is never there when she's needed.

When these words are used as exaggerations, they often provoke defensiveness rather than compassion.

Words like *frequently* and *seldom* can also contribute to confusing observation with evaluation.

Evaluations	Observations
You seldom do what I want.	The last three times I initiated an activity, you said you didn't want to do it.
He frequently comes over.	He comes over at least three times a week.

Summary

The first component of NVC entails the separation of observation from evaluation. When we combine observation with evaluation, others are apt to hear criticism and resist what we are saying. NVC is a process language that discourages static generalizations. Instead, observations are to be made specific to time and context, e.g. "Hank Smith has not scored a goal in 20 games" rather than "Hank Smith is a poor soccer player."

NVC in Action

"The most arrogant speaker we've ever had!"

This dialogue occurred during a workshop I was conducting. About half an hour into my presentation, I paused to invite reactions from the participants. One of them raised a hand and declared, "You're the most arrogant speaker we've ever had!"

I have several options open to me when people address me this way. One option is to take the message personally; I know I'm doing this when I have a strong urge to either grovel, defend myself, or make excuses. Another option (for which I am well-rehearsed) is to attack the other person for what I perceive as their attack upon me. On this occasion, I chose a third option by focusing on what might be going on behind the man's statement.

MBR: *(guessing at the observations he was making)* Are you reacting to my having taken 30 straight minutes to present my views before giving you a chance to talk?

Phil: No, you make it sound so simple.

MBR: *(trying to obtain further clarification)* Are you reacting to my not having said anything about how the process can be difficult for some people to apply?

Phil: No, not some people—you!

MBR: So you're reacting to my not having said that the process can be difficult for me at times?

Phil: That's right.

MBR: Are you feeling annoyed because you would have liked some sign from me that indicated that I have some problems with the process myself?

Phil: (after a moment's pause) That's right.

MBR: (More relaxed now that I am in touch with the person's feeling and need, I direct my attention to what he might be requesting of me) Would you like me to admit right now that this process can be a struggle for me to apply?

Phil: Yes.

MBR: (Having gotten clear on his observation, feeling, need, and request, I check inside myself to see if I am willing to do as he requests) Yes, this process is often difficult for me. As we continue with the workshop, you'll probably hear me describe several incidents where I've struggled . . . or completely lost touch . . . with this process, this consciousness, that I am presenting here to you. But what keeps me in the struggle are the close connections to other people that happen when I do stay with the process.

Exercise 1
OBSERVATION OR EVALUATION?

To determine your proficiency at discerning between observations and evaluations, complete the following exercise. Circle the number in front of any statement that is an observation only, with no evaluation mixed in.

1. "John was angry with me yesterday for no reason."

2. "Yesterday evening Nancy bit her fingernails while watching television."

3. "Sam didn't ask for my opinion during the meeting."

4. "My father is a good man."

5. "Janice works too much."

6. "Henry is aggressive."

7. "Pam was first in line every day this week."

8. "My son often doesn't brush his teeth."

9. "Luke told me I didn't look good in yellow."

10. "My aunt complains when I talk with her."

Here are my responses for Exercise 1:

1. If you circled this number, we're not in agreement. I consider "for no reason" to be an evaluation. Furthermore, I consider it an evaluation to infer that John was angry. He might have been feeling hurt, scared, sad, or something else. Examples of observations without evaluation might be: "John told me he was angry," or "John pounded his fist on the table."

2. If you circled this number, we're in agreement that an observation was expressed without being mixed together with an evaluation.

3. If you circled this number, we're in agreement that an observation was expressed without being mixed together with an evaluation.

4. If you circled this number, we're not in agreement. I consider "good man" to be an evaluation. An observation without evaluation might be: "For the last 25 years my father has given one tenth of his salary to charity."

5. If you circled this number, we're not in agreement. I consider "too much" to be an evaluation. An observation without evaluation might be, "Janice spent over 60 hours at the office this week."

6. If you circled this number, we're not in agreement. I consider "aggressive" to be an evaluation. An observation without evaluation might be: "Henry hit his sister when she switched the television channel."

7. If you circled this number, we're in agreement that an observation was expressed without being mixed together with an evaluation.

8. If you circled this number, we're not in agreement. I consider "often" to be an evaluation. An observation without evaluation might be: "Twice this week my son didn't brush his teeth before going to bed."

9. If you circled this number, we're in agreement that an observation was expressed without being mixed together with an evaluation.

10. If you circled this number, we're not in agreement. I consider "complains" to be an evaluation. An observation without evaluation might be: "My aunt called me three times this week, and each time talked about people who treated her in ways she didn't like."

The Mask

Always a mask
Held in the slim hand whitely
Always she had a mask before her face —

Truly the wrist
Holding it lightly
Fitted the task:
Sometimes however
Was there a shiver,
Fingertip quiver,
Ever so slightly —
Holding the mask?

For years and years and years I wondered
But dared not ask
And then —
I blundered,
looked behind the mask,
To find
Nothing —
She had no face.

She had become
Merely a hand
Holding a mask
With grace.

                            —Author unknown

CHAPTER FOUR

Identifying and Expressing Feelings

The first component of NVC is to observe without evaluating; the second component is to express how we are feeling. Psychoanalyst Rollo May suggests that "the mature person becomes able to differentiate feelings into as many nuances, strong and passionate experiences, or delicate and sensitive ones as in the different passages of music in a symphony." For many of us, however, our feelings are, as May would describe it, "limited like notes in a bugle call."

The Heavy Cost Of Unexpressed Feelings

Our repertoire of words for calling people names is often larger than our vocabulary of words that allow us to clearly describe our emotional states. I went through twenty-one years of American schools and can't recall anyone in all that time ever asking me how I felt. Feelings were simply not considered important. What was valued was "the right way to think"—as defined by those who held positions of rank and authority. We are trained to be "other-directed" rather than to be in contact with ourselves. We learn to be "up in our head" wondering, "What is it that others think is right for me to say and do?"

An interaction I had with a teacher when I was about nine years old demonstrates how alienation from our feelings can begin. Once I hid myself after school in a classroom because some boys were waiting outside to beat me up. A teacher spotted me and asked me to leave the school. When I explained I was afraid to go, she declared, "Big boys don't get frightened." A few years later I received further reinforcement through my participation in athletics. It was typical for coaches to value athletes willing to "give their all" and continue playing no matter how much physical pain they were in. I learned the lesson so well I once continued playing baseball for a month with an untreated broken wrist.

At an NVC workshop, a college student spoke about a roommate who played the stereo so loudly it kept him awake. When asked to express what he felt when this happened, the student replied, "I feel that it isn't right to play music so loud at night." I pointed out that when he followed the word feel with the word that, he was expressing an opinion but not revealing his feelings. Asked to try again to express his feelings, he responded, "I feel, when people do something like that, it's a personality disturbance." I explained that this was still an opinion rather than a feeling. He paused thoughtfully, and then announced with vehemence, "I have no feelings about it whatsoever!"

This student obviously had strong feelings. Unfortunately, he didn't know how to become aware of his feelings, let alone express them. This difficulty in identifying and expressing feelings is common, and in my experience, especially so among lawyers, engineers, police officers, corporate managers, and career military personnel—people whose professional codes discourage them from manifesting emotions. For families, the toll is severe when members are unable to communicate emotions. Country and western singer Reba McIntire wrote a song after her father's death, and titled it "The Greatest Man I Never Knew." In so doing, she undoubtedly expressed the sentiments of many people who were never able to establish the emotional connection they would have liked with their fathers.

I regularly hear statements like, "I wouldn't want you to get the wrong idea—I'm married to a wonderful man—but I never know what he is feeling." One such dissatisfied woman brought her spouse to a workshop, during which she told him, "I feel like I'm married to a wall." The husband then did an excellent imitation of a wall: he sat mute and immobile. Exasperated, she turned to me and exclaimed, "See! This is what happens all the time. He sits and says nothing. It's just like living with a wall."

"It sounds to me like you are feeling lonely and wanting more emotional contact with your husband," I responded. When she agreed, I tried to show how statements such as "I feel like I'm living with a wall" are unlikely to bring her feelings and desires to her husband's attention. In fact, they are more likely to be heard as criticism than an invitation to connect with our feelings. Furthermore, such statements often lead to self-fulfilling prophecies. A husband, for example, hears himself criticized for behaving like a wall; he is hurt and discouraged and doesn't respond, thereby confirming his wife's image of him as a wall.

The benefits of strengthening our feelings vocabulary are evident not only in intimate relationships, but also in the professional world. I was once hired to consult with the members of a technological department of a large Swiss corporation troubled by the discovery that workers in other departments were avoiding them. When asked why, employees from other departments responded, "We hate going there to consult with those people. It's like talking to a bunch of machines!" The problem abated when I spent time with the members of the technological department, encouraging them to express more of their humanness in their communications with co-workers.

In another instance, I was working with the administrators of a hospital who were anxious about a forthcoming meeting with the hospital's physicians. They wanted support for a project that the physicians had only recently turned down by a vote of 17 to 1. The administrators were eager to have me demonstrate how they might use NVC when approaching the physicians.

Assuming the voice of an administrator in a role-playing session, I opened with, "I'm feeling frightened to be bringing up this issue." I chose to start this way because I sensed how frightened the administrators were as they prepared to confront the physicians on this topic again. Before I could continue, one of the administrators stopped me to protest, "You're being unrealistic! We could never tell the physicians that we were frightened."

When I asked why an admission of fear seemed so impossible, he replied without hesitation, "If we admitted we're frightened, then they would just pick us to pieces!" His answer didn't surprise me; I have often heard people say how they cannot imagine ever expressing feelings at their workplace. I was pleased to learn, however, that one of the administrators did decide to risk expressing his vulnerability at the dreaded meeting. Instead of his customary manner of appearing strictly logical, rational and unemotional, he chose to state his feelings together with reasons for wanting the physicians to change their position. He noticed how differently the physicians responded to him. In the end he was amazed and relieved when, instead of being "picked to pieces" by the physicians, they reversed their previous position, voting 17 to 1 to support the project instead. This dramatic turnaround helped the administrators realize and appreciate the potential impact of expressing one's vulnerability—even in the workplace.

> Expressing our vulnerability can help resolve conflicts.

Finally, let me share a personal incident that taught me the effects of hiding our feelings. I was teaching a course in NVC to a group of inner city students. When I walked into the room the first day, the students, who had been enjoying a lively conversation with each other, became quiet. "Good morning!" I greeted. Silence. I felt very uncomfortable, but was afraid to express it. Instead, I proceeded in my most professional manner, "For this class, we will be studying a process of communication that I hope you will find helpful in your relationships at home and with your friends."

I continued to present information about NVC, but no one seemed to be listening. One girl, rummaging through her bag, fished out a file and began vigorously filing her nails. Students near the windows glued their faces to the pane as if fascinated by what was going on in the street below. I felt increasingly more uncomfortable, yet continued to say nothing. Finally, a student who had certainly more courage than I was demonstrating, piped up, "You just hate being with black people, don't you?" I was stunned, yet immediately realized how I had contributed to this student's perception by trying to hide my discomfort.

"I *am* feeling nervous," I admitted, "but not because you are black. My feelings have to do with my not knowing anyone here and wanting to be accepted when I came in the room." This expression of my vulnerability had a pronounced effect on the students. They started to ask questions about me, to tell me things about themselves, and to express curiosity about NVC.

Feelings Versus Non-Feelings

A common confusion generated by the English language is our use of the word *feel* without actually expressing a feeling. For example, in the sentence, "I feel I didn't get a fair deal," the words "I feel" could be more accurately replaced with "I think." In general, feelings are not being clearly expressed when the word *feel* is followed by:

a) words such as *that, like,* as *if*:
  "I feel *that* you should know better."
  "I feel *like* a failure."
  "I feel *as* if I'm living with a wall."

> Distinguish feelings from thoughts.

b) the pronouns *I, you, he, she, they, it*:
  "I feel *I* am constantly on call."
  "I feel *it* is useless."

c) names or nouns referring to people:
  "I feel *Amy* has been pretty responsible."
  "I feel *my boss* is being manipulative."

Conversely, in the English language, it is not necessary at all to use the word *feel* when we are actually expressing a feeling: we can say "I'm feeling irritated," or simply, "I'm irritated."

> Distinguish between WHAT WE FEEL and WHAT WE THINK we are.

In NVC, we distinguish between words that express actual feelings and those that describe *what we think we are.*

A. Description of what we *think* we are:
"I feel *inadequate* as a guitar player."
In this statement, I am assessing my ability as a guitar player, rather than clearly expressing my feelings.

B. Expressions of actual feelings:
"I feel *disappointed* in myself as a guitar player."
"I feel *impatient* with myself as a guitar player."
"I feel *frustrated* with myself as a guitar player."
The actual feeling behind my assessment of myself as "inadequate" could therefore be disappointment, impatience, frustration, or some other emotion.

Likewise, it is helpful to differentiate between words that describe what we think others are doing around us, and words that describe actual feelings. The following are examples of statements that are easily mistaken as expressions of feelings: in fact they reveal more *how we think others are behaving* than what we are actually feeling ourselves:

> Distinguish between WHAT WE FEEL and HOW WE THINK others react or behave toward us.

A. "I feel unimportant to the people with whom I work."
The word *unimportant* describes how I think others are evaluating me, rather than an actual feeling, which in this situation might be "I feel *sad*" or "I feel *discouraged.*"

B. "I feel misunderstood."
Here the word *misunderstood* indicates my assessment of the other person's level of understanding rather than an actual feeling. In this situation, I may be feeling *anxious* or *annoyed* or some other emotion.

C. "I feel *ignored.*"

Again, this is more of an interpretation of the actions of others rather than a clear statement of how we are feeling. No doubt there have been times we thought we were being ignored and our feeling was *relief,* because we wanted to be left to ourselves. No doubt there were other times, however, when we felt *hurt* when we thought we were being ignored, because we had wanted to be involved.

Words like "ignored" express how we *interpret others*, rather than how we *feel*. Here is a sampling of such words.

abandoned	distrusted	put down
abused	interrupted	rejected
attacked	intimidated	taken for granted
betrayed	let down	threatened
boxed-in	manipulated	unappreciated
bullied	misunderstood	unheard
cheated	neglected	unseen
coerced	overworked	unsupported
co-opted	patronized	unwanted
cornered	pressured	used
diminished	provoked	

Building A Vocabulary For Feelings

In expressing our feelings, it helps to use words that refer to specific emotions, rather than words that are vague or general. For example, if we say, "I feel good about that," the word *good* could mean *happy, excited, relieved* or a number of other emotions. Words such as *good* and *bad* prevent the listener from connecting easily with what we might actually be feeling.

The following lists have been compiled to help you increase your power to articulate feelings and clearly describe a whole range of emotional states.

How we are likely to feel when our needs "are" being met

absorbed	engrossed	moved
adventurous	enlivened	optimistic
affectionate	enthusiastic	overjoyed
alert	excited	overwhelmed
alive	exhilarated	peaceful
amazed	expansive	perky
amused	expectant	pleasant
animated	exultant	pleased
appreciative	fascinated	proud
ardent	free	quiet
aroused	fricndly	radiant
astonished	fulfilled	rapturous
blissful	glad	refreshed
breathless	gleeful	relaxed
buoyant	glorious	relieved
calm	glowing	satisfied
carefree	good-humored	secure
cheerful	grateful	sensitive
comfortable	gratified	serene
complacent	happy	spellbound
composed	helpful	splendid
concerned	hopeful	stimulated
confident	inquisitive	surprised
contented	inspired	tender
cool	intense	thankful
curious	interested	thrilled
dazzled	intrigued	touched
delighted	invigorated	tranquil
eager	involved	trusting
ebullient	joyous, joyful	upbeat
ecstatic	jubilant	warm
effervescent	keyed-up	wide-awake
elated	loving	wonderful
enchanted	mellow	zestful
encouraged	merry	
energetic	mirthful	

How we are likely to feel when our needs "are not" being met

afraid	disgusted	intense
aggravated	disheartened	irate
agitated	dismayed	irked
alarmed	displeased	irritated
aloof	disquieted	jealous
angry	distressed	jittery
anguished	disturbed	keyed-up
annoyed	downcast	lazy
anxious	downhearted	leery
apathetic	dull	lethargic
apprehensive	edgy	listless
aroused	embarrassed	lonely
ashamed	embittered	mad
beat	exasperated	mean
bewildered	exhausted	miserable
bitter	fatigued	mopey
blah	fearful	morose
blue	fidgety	mournful
bored	forlorn	nervous
brokenhearted	frightened	nettled
chagrined	frustrated	numb
cold	furious	overwhelmed
concerned	gloomy	panicky
confused	guilty	passive
cool	harried	perplexed
cross	heavy	pessimistic
dejected	helpless	puzzled
depressed	hesitant	rancorous
despairing	horrified	reluctant
despondent	horrible	repelled
detached	hostile	resentful
disaffected	hot	restless
disenchanted	humdrum	sad
disappointed	hurt	scared
discouraged	impatient	sensitive
disgruntled	indifferent	shaky

shocked	terrified	upset
skeptical	tired	uptight
sleepy	troubled	vexed
sorrowful	uncomfortable	weary
sorry	unconcerned	wistful
spiritless	uneasy	withdrawn
startled	unglued	woeful
surprised	unhappy	worried
suspicious	unnerved	wretched
tepid	unsteady	

Summary

The second component necessary for expressing ourselves is feelings. By developing a vocabulary of feelings that allows us to clearly and specifically name or identify our emotions, we can connect more easily with one another. Allowing ourselves to be vulnerable by expressing our feelings can help resolve conflicts. NVC distinguishes the expression of actual feelings from words and statements that describe thoughts, assessments, and interpretations.

Exercise 2
EXPRESSING FEELINGS

If you would like to see whether we're in agreement about the verbal expression of feelings, circle the number in front of any of the following statements in which feelings are verbally expressed.

1. "I feel you don't love me."

2. "I'm sad that you're leaving."

3. "I feel scared when you say that."

4. "When you don't greet me, I feel neglected."

5. "I'm happy that you can come."

6. "You're disgusting."

7. "I feel like hitting you."

8. "I feel misunderstood."

9. "I feel good about what you did for me."

10. "I'm worthless."

Here are my responses for Exercise 2:

1. If you circled this number, we're not in agreement. I don't consider "you don't love me" to be a feeling. To me, it expresses what the speaker thinks the other person is feeling, rather than how the speaker is feeling. Whenever the words "I feel" are followed by the words "I," "you," "he," "she," "they," "it," "that," "like," or "as if," what follows is generally not what I would consider to be a feeling. Examples of an expression of feeling might be: "I'm sad" or "I'm feeling anguished."

2. If you circled this number, we're in agreement that a feeling was verbally expressed.

3. If you circled this number, we're in agreement that a feeling was verbally expressed.

4. If you circled this number, we're not in agreement. I don't consider "neglected" to be a feeling. To me, it expresses what the speaker thinks the other person is doing to him or her. An expression of feeling might be: "When you don't greet me at the door, I feel lonely."

5. If you circled this number, we're in agreement that a feeling was verbally expressed.

6. If you circled this number, we're not in agreement. I don't consider "disgusting" to be a feeling. To me, it expresses how the speaker thinks about the other person, rather than how the speaker is feeling. An expression of feeling might be: "I feel disgusted."

7. If you circled this number, we're not in agreement. I don't consider "like hitting you" to be a feeling. To me, it expresses what the speaker imagines doing, rather than how the speaker is feeling. An expression of feeling might be: "I am furious at you."

8. If you circled this number, we're not in agreement. I don't consider "misunderstood" to be a feeling. To me, it expresses what the speaker thinks the other person is doing. An expression of feeling in this case might be, "I feel frustrated," or "I feel discouraged."

9. If you circled this number, we're in agreement that a feeling was verbally expressed. However, the word "good" is vague when used to convey a feeling. We can usually express our feelings more clearly by using other words, e.g. in this instance: "relieved," "gratified," or "encouraged."

10. If you circled this number, we're not in agreement. I don't consider "worthless" to be a feeling. To me, it expresses how the speaker thinks about him or herself, rather than how the speaker is feeling. Examples of an expression of feeling might be: "I feel skeptical about my own talents," or "I feel wretched."

CHAPTER FIVE

Taking Responsibility For Our Feelings

"People are disturbed not by things, but by the view they take of them."
—Epictetus

Hearing A Negative Message: Four Options

The third component of NVC entails the acknowledgment of the root of our feelings. NVC heightens our awareness that what others say and do may be the *stimulus*, but never the *cause* of

> What others do may be the stimulus of our feelings, but not the cause.

our feelings. We see that our feelings result from how we *choose* to receive what others say and do, as well as our particular needs and expectations in that moment. With the third component, we are led to accept responsibility for what we do to generate our own feelings.

When someone gives us a negative message, whether verbally or nonverbally, we have four options as to how to receive it. One is to take it personally by hearing blame and criticism. For example, someone is angry and says, "You're the most self-centered person I've ever met!" In choosing to take it personally, we might react, "Oh, I should've been more sensitive!" We accept the other person's judgment and blame ourselves. We choose this option

> Four options for receiving negative messages:
> 1. Blaming ourselves

at a great cost to our self-esteem, for it inclines us toward feelings of guilt, shame, and depression.

A second option is to fault the speaker. For example, in response to "You're the most self-centered person I've ever met,"

2. Blaming others

we might protest, "You have no right to say that! I am always considering your needs. You're the one who is really self-centered." When we receive messages this way, and blame the speaker, we are likely to feel anger.

When receiving a negative message, our third option would be to shine the light of consciousness on our own feelings and needs.

3. Sensing our own feelings and needs

Thus, we might reply, "When I hear you saying that I am the most self-centered person you've ever met, I feel hurt, because I need some recognition of my efforts to be considerate of your preferences." By focusing attention on our own feelings and needs, we become conscious that our current feeling of hurt derives from a need for our efforts to be recognized.

Finally, a fourth option in receiving a negative message is to shine the light of consciousness on the *other* person's feelings and

4. Sensing others' feelings and needs

needs as they are currently expressed. We might for example ask, "Are you feeling hurt because you need more consideration for your preferences?"

We accept responsibility rather than blame other people for our feelings by acknowledging our own needs, desires, expectations, values, or thoughts. Note the difference between the following expressions of disappointment:

Example 1

   A: "You disappointed me by not coming over last evening."
   B: "I was disappointed when you didn't come over, because I
      wanted to talk over some things that were bothering me."

Speaker A attributes responsibility for the disappointment solely to the action of the other person. In B, the feeling of disappointment is traced to the speaker's own desire that was not being fulfilled.

Example 2
A: "Their cancelling the contract really irritated me!"
B: "When they cancelled the contract, I felt really irritated because I was thinking to myself that it was an awfully irresponsible thing to do."

Speaker A attributes her irritation solely to the behavior of the other party, whereas Speaker B accepts responsibility for her feeling by acknowledging the thought behind it. She recognizes that her blaming way of thinking has generated her irritation. In NVC, however, we would urge this speaker to go a step further by identifying what she is wanting: what need, desire, expectation, hope, or value of hers has not been fulfilled? As we shall see, the more we are able to connect our feelings to our own needs, the easier it is for others to respond compassionately. To relate her feelings to what she is wanting, Speaker B might have said:

"When they cancelled the contract, I felt really irritated because I was hoping for an opportunity to re-hire the workers we had laid off last year."

> Distinguish between giving from the heart and being motivated out of guilt.

The basic mechanism of motivating by guilt is to attribute the responsibility for one's own feelings to others. When parents say, "It hurts Mommy and Daddy when you get poor grades at school," they are implying that the child's actions are the cause of the parents' happiness or unhappiness. On the surface, feeling responsible for the feelings of others can easily be mistaken for positive caring. It appears that the child cares for the parent and feels bad because the parent is suffering. However, if children who assume this kind of responsibility change their behavior in accordance to parental wishes, they are not acting from the heart, but acting to avoid guilt.

It is helpful to recognize a number of common speech patterns that tend to mask accountability for our own feelings:

1) Use of impersonal pronouns such as "it" and "that": "It really infuriates me when spelling mistakes appear in our public brochures." "That bugs me a lot."

2) Statements that mention only the actions of others:
"When you don't call me on my birthday, I feel hurt." "Mommy is disappointed when you don't finish your food."

3) The use of the expression "I feel (an emotion) because . . . " followed by a person or personal pronoun other than "I":
"I feel hurt because you said you don't love me." "I feel angry because the supervisor broke her promise."

> Connect your feeling with your need: "I feel . . . because I . . ."

In each of these instances, we can deepen our awareness of our own responsibility by substituting the phrase, "I feel . . . because I . . . " For example:

1) "*I feel* really infuriated when spelling mistakes like that appear in our public brochures, *because I* want our company to project a professional image."

2) "*Mommy feels* disappointed when you don't finish your food, *because I* want you to grow up strong and healthy."

3) "*I feel* angry that the supervisor broke her promise, *because I* was counting on getting that long weekend to visit my brother."

The Needs At The Roots Of Feelings

> Judgments of others are alienated expressions of our own unmet needs.

Judgments, criticisms, diagnoses, and interpretations of others are all alienated expressions of our needs. If someone says, "You never understand me," they are really telling us that their need to be understood is not being fulfilled. If a wife says, "You've been working late every night this week; you love your work more than you love me," she is saying that her need for intimacy is not being met.

When we express our needs indirectly through the use of evaluations, interpretations, and images, others are likely to hear criticism. And when people hear anything that sounds like criticism, they tend to invest their energy in self-defense or counterattack. If we are wishing for a compassionate response from others, it is self-defeating to express our needs by interpreting or diagnosing their behavior. Instead, the more directly we can connect our feelings to our own needs, the easier it is for others to respond compassionately to our needs.

> If we express our needs, we have a better chance of getting them met.

Unfortunately, most of us have never been taught to think in terms of needs. We are accustomed to thinking about what's wrong with other people when our needs aren't being fulfilled. Thus, if we want coats to be hung up in the closet, we may characterize our children as lazy for leaving them on the couch. Or we may interpret our co-workers as being irresponsible when they don't go about their tasks as we would prefer them to.

I was once invited to mediate in southern California between some landowners and migrant farm workers whose conflicts had grown increasingly hostile and violent. I began the meeting by asking them two questions: "What is it that you are each needing? And what would you like to request of the other in relation to these needs?" "The problem is that these people are racist!" shouted a farm worker. "The problem is that these people don't respect law and order!" shouted a landowner even more loudly. As is often the case, these groups were more skilled in analyzing the perceived wrongness of others than in clearly expressing their own needs.

In a comparable situation, I once met with a group of Israelis and Palestinians who wanted to establish the mutual trust necessary to bring peace to their homelands. I opened the session with the same questions, "What is it you are needing and what would you like to request from one another in relation to those needs?" Instead of directly stating his needs, a Palestinian mukhtar (who is like a village mayor) answered, "You people are acting like a bunch of Nazis." A statement like that is not likely to get the cooperation of a group of Israelis!

Almost immediately, an Israeli woman jumped up and countered, "Mukhtar, that was a totally insensitive thing for you to say!" Here were people who had come together to build trust and harmony, but after only one interchange, matters were worse than before they began. This happens often when people are used to analyzing and blaming one another rather than clearly expressing what they need. In this case, the woman could have responded to the Mukhtar in terms of her own needs and requests by saying, for example, "I am needing more respect in our dialogue. Instead of telling us how you think we are acting, would you tell us what it is we are doing that you find disturbing?"

Over and over again, it has been my experience that, from the moment people begin talking about what they need rather than what's wrong with one another, the possibility of finding ways to meet everybody's needs is greatly increased. The following are some of the basic human needs we all share:

Autonomy
- to choose one's dreams, goals, values
- to choose one's plan for fulfilling one's dreams, goals, values

Celebration
- to celebrate the creation of life and dreams fulfilled
- to celebrate losses: loved ones, dreams, etc. (mourning)

Integrity
- authenticity
- creativity
- meaning
- self-worth

Interdependence
- acceptance
- appreciation
- closeness
- community
- consideration
- contribution to the enrichment of life (to exercise

one's power by giving that which contributes to life)
- emotional safety
- empathy
- honesty (the empowering honesty that enables us to learn from our limitations)
- love
- reassurance
- respect
- support
- trust
- understanding
- warmth

Play
- fun
- laughter

Spiritual Communion
- beauty
- harmony
- inspiration
- order
- peace

Physical Nurturance
- air
- food
- movement, exercise
- protection from life-threatening forms of life: viruses, bacteria, insects, predatory animals
- rest
- sexual expression
- shelter
- touch
- water

The Pain Of Expressing Our Needs Versus The Pain Of Not Expressing Our Needs

In a world where we're often judged harshly for identifying and revealing our needs, doing so can be very frightening. Women, in particular, are susceptible to criticism. For centuries, the image of the loving woman has been associated with sacrifice and the denial of her own needs to take care of others. Because women are social-ized to view the care taking of others as their highest duty, they have often learned to ignore their own needs.

At one workshop, we discussed what happens to women who internalize such beliefs. These women, if they ask for what they want, will often do so in a way that both reflects and reinforces the beliefs that they have no genuine right to their needs, and that their needs are unimportant. For example, because she is fearful of asking for what she needs, a woman may fail to simply say that she's had a busy day, is feeling tired and wants some time in the evening to herself; instead, her words come out sounding like a legal case: "You know I haven't had a moment to myself all day, I ironed all the shirts, did the whole week's laundry, took the dog to the vet, made dinner, packed the lunches, and called all the neighbors about the block meeting, so [imploringly] . . . so how about if you . . . ?" "No!" comes the swift response. Her plaintive request elicits resistance rather than compassion from her listeners. They have difficulty hearing and valuing the needs behind her pleas, and furthermore react negatively to her weak attempt to argue from a position of what she "should" or "deserves" to get from them. In the end the speaker is again persuaded that her needs don't matter, not realizing that they were expressed in a way unlikely to draw a positive response.

If we don't value our needs, others may not either.

My mother was once at a workshop where other women were discussing how frightening it was to be expressing their needs. Suddenly she got up and left the room and didn't return for a long time. She finally reappeared, looking very pale. In the presence of the group, I asked, "Mother, are you all right?"

"Yes," she answered, "but I just had a sudden realization that's very hard for me to take in."

"What's that?"

"I've just become aware that I was angry for 36 years with your father for not meeting my needs, and now I realize that I never once clearly told him what I needed."

My mother's revelation was accurate. Not one time can I remember her clearly expressing her needs to my father. She'd hint around and go through all kinds of convolutions, but never would she ask directly for what she needed.

We tried to understand why it was so hard for her to have done so. My mother grew up in an economically impoverished family. She recalled asking for things as a child and being admonished by her brothers and sisters, "You shouldn't ask for that! You know we're poor. Do you think you are the only person in the family?" Eventually she grew to fear that asking for what she needed would only lead to disapproval and judgment.

She related a childhood anecdote about one of her sisters who had had an appendix operation and afterwards had been given a beautiful little purse by another sister. My mother was 14 at the time. Oh, how she yearned to have an exquisitely beaded purse like her sister's, but she dared not open her mouth. So guess what? She feigned a pain in her side and went the whole way with her story. Her family took her to several doctors. They were unable to produce a diagnosis and so opted for exploratory surgery. It had been a bold gamble on my mother's part, but it worked—she was given an identical little purse! When she received the coveted purse, my mother was elated despite being in physical agony from the surgery. Two nurses came in and one stuck a thermometer in her mouth. My mother said, "Ummm, ummm," to show the purse to the second nurse, who answered, "Oh, for me? Why, thank you!" and took the purse! My mother was at a loss, and never figured out how to say, "I didn't mean to give it to you. Please return it to me." Her story poignantly reveals how painful it can be when people don't openly acknowledge their needs.

From Emotional Slavery To Emotional Liberation

In our development toward a state of emotional liberation, most of us seem to experience three stages in the way we relate to others.

Stage 1: In this stage, which I refer to as *emotional slavery*, we believe ourselves responsible for the feelings of others. We think we must constantly strive to keep everyone happy. If they don't appear happy, we feel responsible and compelled to do something about it. This can easily lead us to see the very people who are closest to us as burdens.

Taking responsibility for the feelings of others can be very detrimental in intimate relationships. I routinely hear variations on the following theme: "I'm really scared to be in a relationship.

First stage: Emotional slavery: we see ourselves responsible for others' feelings.

Every time I see my partner in pain or needing something, I feel overwhelmed. I feel like I'm in prison, that I'm being smothered—and I just have to get out of the relationship as fast as possible." This response is common among those who experience love as denial of one's own needs in order to attend to the needs of the beloved. In the early days of a relationship, partners typically relate joyfully and compassionately to each other out of a sense of freedom. The relationship is exhilarating, spontaneous, wonderful. Eventually, however, as the relationship becomes "serious," partners may begin to assume responsibility for each other's feelings.

If I were a partner who is conscious of doing this, I might acknowledge the situation by explaining, "I can't bear it when I lose myself in relationships. When I see my partner's pain, I lose me, and then I just have to break free." However, if I have not reached this level of awareness, I am likely to blame my partner for the deterioration of the relationship. Thus I might say, "My partner is so needy and dependent it's really stressing out our relationship." In such a case, my partner would do well to reject the notion that there is anything wrong with her needs. It would only make a bad situation worse to accept that blame. Instead, she could offer an empathic response to address the pain of my emotional slavery: "So you find yourself in panic. It's very hard for you to hold on to the deep caring and love we've had without turning it into a responsibility, duty, obligation. . . . You sense your freedom closing down because you think you constantly have to take care of me." If, however, instead of an empathic response, she says, "Are you feeling tense because I have been making too many demands on you?" then both of us are likely to stay enmeshed in emotional slavery, making it that much more difficult for the relationship to survive.

Stage 2: In this stage, we become aware of the high costs of assuming responsibility for others' feelings and trying to accommodate them at our own expense. When we notice how much of our lives we've missed and how little we have responded to the call of our own soul, we may get angry. I refer jokingly to this stage as the *obnoxious stage* because we tend toward obnoxious comments like, "That's *your* problem! *I'm* not respon-

sible for your feelings!" when presented with another person's pain. We are clear what we are not responsible *for*, but have yet to learn how to be responsible *to* others in a way that is not emotionally enslaving.

As we emerge from the stage of emotional enslavement, we may continue to carry remnants of fear and guilt around having our own needs. Thus it is not surprising that we end up expressing those needs in ways that sound rigid and unyielding to the ears of others. For example, during a break in one of my workshops, a young woman expressed appreciation for the insights she'd gained into her own state of emotional enslavement. When the workshop resumed, I suggested an activity to the group. The same young woman then declared assertively, "I'd rather do something else." I sensed she was exercising her newfound right to express her needs—even if they ran counter to those of others.

To encourage her to sort out what she wanted, I asked, "Do you want to do something else even if it conflicts with my needs?" She thought for a moment, and then stammered, "Yes. . . . er . . . I mean no." Her confusion reflects how, in the obnoxious stage, we have yet to grasp that emotional liberation entails more than simply asserting our own needs.

I recall an incident during my daughter Marla's passage toward emotional liberation. She had always been the "perfect little girl" who denied her own needs to comply with the wishes of others. When I became aware of how frequently she suppressed her own desires in order to please others, I talked to her about how I'd enjoy hearing her express her needs more often. When we first broached the subject, Marla cried. "But, Daddy, I don't want to disappoint anybody!" she protested helplessly. I tried to show Marla how her honesty would be a gift more precious to others than accommodating them to prevent their upset. I also clarified ways she could empathize with people when they were upset without taking responsibility for their feelings.

A short time later, I saw evidence that my daughter was beginning to express her needs more openly. A call came from her school principal, apparently disturbed by a communication he'd had with Marla, who had arrived at school wearing overalls. "Marla," he'd said, "young women do not dress this way." To which Marla had responded, "F___ off!" Hearing this was cause for celebration: Marla had graduated from emotional slavery to obnoxiousness! She was learning to express her needs and risk dealing with the displeasure of others. Surely she had yet to assert her needs comfortably and in a way that respected the needs of others, but I trusted this would occur in time.

Stage 3: At the third stage, *emotional liberation*, we respond to the needs of others out of compassion, never out of fear, guilt, or shame. Our actions are therefore fulfilling to us, as well as to those who receive our efforts. We accept full responsibility for our own intentions and actions, but not for the feelings of others. At this stage, we are aware that we can never meet our own needs at the expense of others. Emotional liberation involves stating clearly what we need in a way that communicates we are equally concerned that the needs of others be fulfilled. NVC is designed to support us in relating at this level.

> Third stage: Emotional liberation: we take responsibility for our intentions and actions

Summary

The third component of NVC is the acknowledgment of the needs behind our feelings. What others say and do may be the *stimulus*, but never the cause, of our feelings. When someone communicates negatively, we have four options as to how to receive the message: (1) blame ourselves, (2) blame others, (3) sense our own feelings and needs, (4) sense the feelings and needs hidden in the other person's negative message.

Judgments, criticisms, diagnoses, and interpretations of others are all alienated expressions of our own needs and values. When others hear criticism, they tend to invest their energy in self-defense or counterattack. The more directly we can connect our feelings to our needs, the easier it is for others to respond compassionately.

In a world where we are often harshly judged for identifying and revealing our needs, doing so can be very frightening, especially for women who are socialized to ignore their own needs while caring for others.

In the course of developing emotional responsibility, most of us experience three stages: (1) "emotional slavery"—believing ourselves responsible for the feelings of others, (2) "the obnoxious stage"—in which we refuse to admit to caring what anyone else feels or needs, and (3) "emotional liberation"—in which we accept full responsibility for our own feelings but not the feelings of others, while being aware that we can never meet our own needs at the expense of others.

NVC in Action

"Bring back the stigma of illegitimacy!"

A student of Nonviolent Communication volunteering at a food bank was shocked when an elderly co-worker bursts out from behind a newspaper, "What we need to do in this country is to bring back the stigma of illegitimacy!"

The woman's habitual reaction to this kind of statement would have been to say nothing, to judge the other severely but silently, and eventually process her own feelings safely away from the scene. This time she remembered she had the option of listening for the feelings and needs behind the words that had shocked her.

Woman:	*(first checking out her guess as to what the co-worker was observing)* Are you reading something about teenage pregnancies in the paper?
Co-worker:	Yes, it's unbelievable how many of them are doing it!
Woman:	*(now listening for the co-worker's feeling, and what unmet need might be giving rise to this feeling)* Are you feeling alarmed because you'd like kids to have stable families?
Co-worker:	Of course! Do you know, my father would have killed me if I had done anything like that!
Woman:	So you're remembering how it was for the girls in your generation who got pregnant?
Co-worker:	Sure thing! We knew what would happen to us if we got pregnant. We were scared about it all the time, not like these girls nowadays.
Woman:	Are you annoyed that there is no fear of punishment for the girls who get pregnant these days?
Co-worker:	Well, at least fear and punishment worked! It says here that there are girls sleeping around with different men just so they can get pregnant! That's right! They have babies and the rest of us in society pay for it!

The woman heard two different feelings in this statement: astonishment that girls would deliberately get pregnant, and annoyance that taxpayers end up paying for children born in this way. She chose which feeling to empathize with.

Woman:	Are you astonished to realize that people are getting pregnant these days without any consideration for reputation, consequences, financial stability . . . all the things you used to consider?

Co-worker: *(Feeling heard around her astonishment, she now moved to her other feeling, that of annoyance. As often happens when there is a mixture of feelings present, the speaker will return to those that have not received empathic attention. It is not necessary for the listener to reflect back a complex mixture of feelings all at once; the flow of compassion will continue as each feeling comes up again in its turn)* Yeah, and guess who ends up paying for it?

Woman: Sounds like you're exasperated because you'd like your tax money to be used for other purposes. Is that so?

Co-worker: Certainly is! Do you know that my son and his wife want a second child and they can't have one — even though they have two jobs — because it costs so much?

Woman: I guess you're sad about that? You'd probably love to have a second grandchild . . .

Co-worker: Yes, and it's not just for me that it would make a difference.

Woman: . . . and for your son to have the family he wants . . . *(Even though the woman guessed only partially correctly, she did not interrupt the flow of empathy, allowing the co-worker to continue and realize another concern.)*

Co-worker: Yes, I think it's sad to be a single child too.

Woman: Oh, I see; you'd like for Katie to have a little brother?

Co-worker: That would be nice.

At this point, the woman sensed a release in her co-worker. A moment of silence elapsed. The woman felt surprised to discover that, while she still wanted to express her own views, the urgency and tension had dissipated because *she no longer felt "adversarial." She understood the feelings and needs behind her co-worker's statements and no longer felt that the two of them were "worlds apart."*

Woman:	You know, when you first said that we should bring back the stigma of illegitimacy (O), I got really scared (F), because it really matters to me that all of us here share a deep caring for people needing help (N). Some of the people coming here for food are teenaged parents (O), and I want to make sure they feel welcome (N). Would you mind telling me how you feel when you see Dashal or Amy and her boyfriend walking in? (R)

The woman expressed herself in NVC, using all four parts of the process: observation (O), feeling (F), need (N), request (R).

The dialogue continued with several more exchanges until the woman got the reassurance she needed that her co-worker did indeed offer caring and respectful help to unmarried teen clients. Even more importantly, what the woman gained was a new experience in expressing disagreement in a way that met her needs for honesty and mutual respect.

In the meantime, the co-worker left satisfied that her concerns around teen pregnancy had been fully heard. Both parties felt understood and their relationship benefited from their having shared their understanding and differences without hostility. In the absence of NVC, their relationship might have begun to deteriorate from this moment, and the work they both wanted to do in common—taking care and helping people—might have suffered.

Exercise 3
ACKNOWLEDGING NEEDS

To practice identifying needs, please circle the number in front of any statement whereby the speaker is acknowledging responsibility for his or her feelings.

1. "You irritate me when you leave company documents on the conference room floor."

2. "I feel angry when you say that, because I am wanting respect and I hear your words as an insult."

3. "I feel frustrated when you come late."

4. "I'm sad that you won't be coming for dinner because I was hoping we could spend the evening together."

5. "I feel disappointed because you said you would do it and you didn't."

6. "I'm discouraged because I would have liked to have progressed further in my work by now."

7. "Little things people say sometimes hurt me."

8. "I feel happy that you received that award."

9. "I feel scared when you raise your voice."

10. "I am grateful that you offered me a ride because I was needing to get home before my children."

Here are my responses for Exercise 3:

1. If you circled this number, we're not in agreement. To me, the statement implies that the other person's behavior is solely responsible for the speaker's feelings. It doesn't reveal the speaker's needs or thoughts that are contributing to his or her feelings. To do so, the speaker might have said, "I'm irritated when you leave company documents on the conference room floor, because I want our documents to be safely stored and accessible."

2. If you circled this number, we're in agreement that the speaker is acknowledging responsibility for his or her feelings.

3. If you circled this number, we're not in agreement. To express the needs or thoughts underlying his or her feelings, the speaker might have said, "I feel frustrated when you come late because I was hoping we'd be able to get some front-row seats."

4. If you circled this number, we're in agreement that the speaker is acknowledging responsibility for his or her feelings.

5. If you circled this number, we're not in agreement. To express the needs and thoughts underlying his or her feelings, the speaker might have said, "When you said you'd do it and then didn't, I feel disappointed because I want to be able to rely upon your words."

6. If you circled this number, we're in agreement that the speaker is acknowledging responsibility for his or her feelings.

7. If you circled this number, we're not in agreement. To express the needs and thoughts underlying his or her feelings, the speaker might have said, "Sometimes when people say little things, I feel hurt because I want to be appreciated, not criticized."

8. If you circled this number, we are not in agreement. To express the needs and thoughts underlying his or her feelings, the speaker might have said, "When you received that award, I felt happy because I was hoping you'd be recognized for all the work you'd put into the project."

9. If you circled this number, we're not in agreement. To express the needs and thoughts underlying his or her feelings, the speaker might have said, "When you raise your voice, I feel scared because I'm telling myself someone might get hurt here, and I need to know that we're all safe."

10. If you circled this number, we're in agreement that the speaker is acknowledging responsibility for his or her feelings.

CHAPTER SIX

Requesting That Which Would Enrich Life

We have now covered the first three components of NVC that address what we are *observing*, *feeling*, and *needing*. We have learned to do this without criticizing, analyzing, blaming, or diagnosing others, and in a way most likely to inspire compassion. The fourth and final component of this process addresses the question of *what we would like to request of others* in order to enrich life for us. When our needs are not being fulfilled, we follow the expression of what we are observing, feeling, and needing with a specific request: we ask for actions that might fulfill our needs. How do we express our requests so that others are more willing to respond compassionately to our needs?

Using Positive Action Language

First of all, we express what we *are* requesting rather than what we *are not* requesting. "How do you do a *don't*?" goes a line of a children's song by my colleague, Ruth Bebermeyer, "All I know is I feel *won't* when I'm told to do a *don't*." These lyrics reveal two problems commonly encountered when requests are worded in the negative. People are often confused as to what is actually being requested, and furthermore, negative requests are likely to provoke resistance.

A woman at a workshop, frustrated that her husband was spending so much time at work, described how her request had

> Use positive language when making requests.

backfired: "I asked him not to spend so much time at work. Three weeks later, he responded by announcing that he'd signed up for a golf tournament!" She had successfully communicated to him what she did not want—his spending so much time at work—but had failed to request what she *did* want. Encouraged to reword her request, she thought a minute and said, "I wish I had told him that I would like him to spend at least one evening a week at home with the children and me."

During the Vietnam War, I was asked to debate the war issue on television with a man whose position differed from mine. The show was videotaped, so I was able to watch it at home that evening. When I saw myself on the screen communicating in ways I didn't want to be communicating, I felt very upset. "If I'm ever in another discussion," I told myself, "I am determined not to do what I did on that program! I'm not going to be defensive. I'm not going to let them make a fool of me." Notice how I spoke to myself in terms of what I *didn't* want to do rather than in terms of what I *did* want to do.

A chance to redeem myself came the very next week when I was invited to continue the debate on the same program. All the way to the studio, I repeated to myself all the things I didn't want to do. As soon as the program started, the man launched off in exactly the same way as he had a week earlier. For about ten seconds after he'd finished talking, I managed not to communicate in the ways I had been reminding myself. In fact, I said nothing. I just sat there. As soon as I opened my mouth, however, I found words tumbling out in all the ways I had been so determined to avoid! It was a painful lesson about what can happen when I only identify what I *don't* want to do, without clarifying what I *do* want to do.

I was once invited to work with some high school students who suffered a long litany of grievances against their principal. They regarded the principal as a racist, and searched for ways to get even with him. A minister who worked closely with the young people became deeply concerned over the prospect of violence. Out of respect for the minister, the students agreed to meet with me.

They began by describing what they saw as discrimination on

the part of the principal. After listening to several of their charges, I suggested that they proceed by clarifying what they wanted from the principal.

"What good would that do?" scoffed one student in disgust, "We already went to him to tell him what we wanted. His answer to us was, 'Get out of here! I don't need you people telling me what to do!'"

I asked the students what they had requested of the principal. They recalled saying to him that they didn't want him telling them how to wear their hair. I suggested that they might have received a more cooperative response if they had expressed what they *did*, rather than what they *did not*, want. They had then informed the principal that they wanted to be treated with fairness, at which he had become defensive, vociferously denying ever having been unfair. I ventured to guess that the principal would have responded more favorably if they had asked for specific actions rather than vague behavior like "fair treatment."

Working together, we found ways to express their requests in positive action language. At the end of the meeting, the students had clarified 38 actions they wanted the principal to take, including "We'd like you to agree to black student representation on decisions made about dress code," and "We'd like you to refer to us as 'black students' and not 'you people.'" The following day, the students presented their requests to the principal using the positive action language we had practiced; that evening I received an elated phone call from them: their principal had agreed to all 38 requests!

In addition to using positive language, we also want to avoid vague, abstract, or ambiguous phrasing and to word our requests in the form of concrete actions that others can undertake. A cartoon depicts a man who has fallen into a lake. As he struggles to swim, he shouts to his dog on shore, "Lassie, get help!" In the next frame, the dog is lying on a psychiatrist's couch. We all know how opinions vary as to what constitutes "help": some members of my family, when asked to help with the dishes, think "help" means supervision.

A couple in distress attending a workshop provides an additional illustration of how nonspecific language can hamper understanding and communication. "I want you to let me be me," the woman declared to her husband. "I do!" he retorted. "No, you don't!" she insisted. Asked to express herself in positive action language, the woman replied, "I want you to give me the freedom to grow and be myself." Such a statement, however, is just as vague and likely to provoke a defensive response. She struggled to formulate her request clearly, and then admitted, "It's kind of awkward, but if I were to be precise, I guess what I want is for you to smile and say that anything I do is okay." Often, the use of vague and abstract language can mask such oppressive interpersonal games.

> Making requests in clear, positive, concrete action language reveals what we really want.

A similar lack of clarity occurred between a father and his 15-year-old son when they came in for counseling. "All I want is for you to start showing a little responsibility," claimed the father. "Is that asking too much?" I suggested that he specify what it would take for his son to demonstrate the responsibility he was seeking. After a discussion on how to clarify his request, the father responded sheepishly, "Well, it doesn't sound so good, but when I say that I want responsibility, what I really mean is that I want him to do what I ask, without question—to jump when I say jump, and to smile while doing it." He then agreed with me that if his son were to actually behave this way, it would demonstrate obedience rather than responsibility.

Like this father, we often use vague and abstract language to indicate how we want other people to feel or be without naming a concrete action they can take to reach that state. For example, an employer makes a genuine effort to invite feedback, telling the employees, "I want you to feel free to express yourself around me." The statement communicates the employer's desire for the employees to "feel free," but not what they could do in order to feel this way. Instead, the employer could use

> Vague language contributes to internal confusion.

positive action language to make a request: "I'd like you to *tell* me what I might *do* to make it easier for you to feel free to express yourselves around me."

As a final illustration of how the use of vague language contributes to internal confusion, I would like to present a conversation that I would invariably have during my practice as a clinical psychologist with the many clients who came to me with complaints of depression. After I empathized with the depth of feelings that a client had just expressed, our exchanges would typically proceed in the following manner:

> **Depression is the reward we get for being "good."**

> *MBR:* "What are you wanting that you are not receiving?"
>
> *Client:* "I don't know what I want."
>
> *MBR:* "I guessed that you would say that."
>
> *Client:* "Why?"
>
> *MBR:* "My theory is that we get depressed because we're not getting what we want, and we're not getting what we want because we have never been taught to get what we want. Instead, we've been taught to be good little boys and girls and good mothers and fathers. If we're going to be one of those good things, better get used to being depressed. Depression is the reward we get for being 'good.' But, if you want to feel better, I'd like you to clarify what you would like people to do to make life more wonderful for you."
>
> *Client:* "I just want someone to love me. That's hardly unreasonable, is it?"
>
> *MBR:* "It's a good start. Now I'd like you to clarify what you would like people to do that would fulfill your need to be loved. For example, what could I do right now?"
>
> *Client:* "Oh, you know . . . "
>
> *MBR:* "I'm not sure I do. I'd like you to tell me what you would like me, or others, to do to give you the love you're looking for."

Client: "That's hard."

MBR: "Yes, it can be difficult to make clear requests. But think how hard it will be for others to respond to our request if we're not even clear what it is!"

Client: "I'm starting to get clear what I want from others to fulfill my need for love, but it's embarrassing."

MBR: "Yes, very often it is embarrassing. So what would you like for me or others to do?"

Client: "If I really reflect upon what I'm requesting when I ask to be loved, I suppose I want you to guess what I want before I'm even aware of it. And then I want you to always do it."

MBR: "I'm grateful for your clarity. I hope you can see how you are not likely to find someone who can fulfill your need for love if that's what it takes."

Very often, my clients were able to see how the lack of awareness of what they wanted from others had contributed significantly to their frustrations and depression.

Making Requests Consciously

Sometimes we may be able to communicate a clear request without putting it in words. Suppose you're in the kitchen and your sister, who is watching television in the living room, calls out, "I'm thirsty." In this case, it may be obvious that she is requesting you to bring her a glass of water from the kitchen.

However, in other instances, we may express our discomfort and incorrectly assume that the listener has understood the underlying request. For example, a woman might say to her husband, "I'm annoyed you forgot the butter and onions I asked you to pick up for dinner." While it may be obvious to her that she is asking him to go back to the store, the husband may think that her words were uttered

> It may not be clear to the listener what we want them to do when we simply express our feelings.

solely to make him feel guilty.

Even more often, we are simply not conscious of what we are requesting when we speak. We talk *to* others or *at* them without knowing how to engage in a dialogue *with* them. We toss out words, using the presence of others as a wastebasket. In such situations, the listener, unable to discern a clear request in the speaker's words, may experience the kind of distress illustrated in the following anecdote.

> We are often not conscious of what we are requesting.

I was seated directly across the aisle from a couple on a minitrain that carries passengers to their respective terminals at the Dallas/Fort Worth Airport. For passengers in a hurry to catch a plane, the snail's pace of the train may well be irritating. The man turned to his wife and said with intensity, "I have never seen a train go so slow in all my life!" She said nothing, appearing tense and uneasy as to what response he might be expecting from her. He then did what many of us do when we're not getting the response we want: he repeated himself. In a markedly stronger voice, he exclaimed, "I have never seen a train go so slow in all my life!"

The wife, at a loss for response, looked even more distressed. In desperation, she turned to him and said, "They're electronically timed." I didn't think this piece of information would satisfy him, and indeed it did not, for he repeated himself a third time—even more loudly, "*I HAVE NEVER SEEN A TRAIN GO SO SLOW IN ALL MY LIFE*!" The wife's patience was clearly exhausted as she snapped back angrily, "Well, what do you want me to do about it? Get out and push?" Now there were two people in pain!

What response was the man wanting? I believe he wanted to hear that his pain was understood. If his wife had known this, she might have responded, "It sounds like you're scared we might miss our plane, and disgusted because you'd like a faster train running between these terminals."

> Requests unaccompanied by the speaker's feelings and needs may sound like a demand.

In the above exchange, the wife heard the husband's frustration but was clueless as to what he was asking for. Equally problematic is the reverse situation—when people state their requests without first communicating the feelings and needs behind them. This is especially true when the request takes the form of a question. "Why don't you go and get a haircut?" can easily be heard by youngsters as a demand or an attack unless parents remember to first reveal their own feelings and needs: "We're worried that your hair is getting so long it might keep you from seeing things, especially when you're on your bike. How about a haircut?"

It is more common, however, for people to talk without being conscious of what they are asking for. "I'm not requesting anything," they might remark, "I just felt like saying what I said." My belief is that, whenever we say something to another person, we are requesting something in return. It may simply be an empathic connection—a verbal or nonverbal acknowledgment, as with the man on the train, that our words have been understood. Or we may be requesting honesty: we wish to know the listener's honest reaction to our words. Or we may be requesting an action that we hope would fulfill our needs. The clearer we are on what we want back from the other person, the more likely it is that our needs will be met.

> The clearer we are about what we want back, the more likely it is that we'll get it.

Asking For A Reflection

As we know, the message we send is not always the message that's received. We generally rely on verbal cues to determine whether our message has been understood to our satisfaction. If, however, we're uncertain that it has been received as intended, we need to be able to clearly request a response that tells us how the message was heard so as to be able to correct any misunderstanding. On some occasions, a simple question like, "Is that clear?" will suffice. At other times, we need more

> To make sure the message we sent is the message that's received, ask the listener to reflect it back.

than "Yes, I understood you," to feel confident that we've been truly understood. At such times, we might ask others to reflect back in their own words what they heard us say. We then have the opportunity to restate parts of our message to address any discrepancy or omission we might have noticed in their reflection.

For example, a teacher approaches a student and says, "Peter, I got concerned when I checked my record book yesterday. I want to make sure you're aware of the homework I'm missing from you. Will you drop by my office after school?" Peter mumbles, "Okay, I know" and then turns away, leaving the teacher uneasy as to whether her message had been accurately received. She asks for a reflection—"Could you tell me what you just heard me say?"—to which Peter replies, "You said I gotta miss soccer to stay after school because you didn't like my homework." Confirmed in her suspicion that Peter had not heard her intended message, the teacher tries to restate it, but first she is careful of her next remark.

> Express appreciation when your listener tries to meet your request for a reflection.

An assertion like "You didn't hear me," "That's not what I said," or "You're misunderstanding me," may easily lead Peter to think that he is being chastised. Since the teacher perceives Peter as having sincerely responded to her request for a reflection, she might say, "I'm grateful to you for telling me what you heard. I can see that I didn't make myself as clear as I'd have liked, so let me try again."

When we first begin asking others to reflect back what they hear us say, it may feel awkward and strange because such requests are rarely made. When I emphasize the importance of our ability to ask for reflections, people often express reservations. They are worried about reactions like, "What do you think I am—deaf?" or "Quit playing your psychological games." To prevent such responses, we can explain to people ahead of time why we may sometimes ask them to reflect back our words. We make clear that we're not testing their listening

> Empathize with the listener who doesn't want to reflect back.

skills, but checking out whether we've expressed ourselves clearly. However, should the listener retort, "I heard what you said; I'm not stupid!", we have the option to focus on their feelings and needs and ask—either aloud or silently, "Are you saying you're feeling annoyed because you want respect for your ability to understand things?"

Requesting Honesty

After we've openly expressed ourselves and received the understanding we want, we're often eager to know the other person's reaction to what we've said. Usually the honesty we would like to receive takes one of three directions:

> After we express ourselves vulnerably, we often want to know (a) what the listener is feeling;

- Sometimes we'd like to know the feelings that are stimulated by what we said, and the reasons for those feelings. We might request this by asking, "I would like you to tell me how you feel about what I just said, and your reasons for feeling as you do."

- Sometimes we'd like to know something about our listener's thoughts in response to what they just heard us say. At these times, it's important to specify which thoughts we'd like them to share. For example, we might say, "I'd like you to tell me if you predict that my proposal would be successful, and if not, what you believe would prevent its success,"

> (b) what the listener is thinking; or

rather than simply saying, "I'd like you to tell me what you think about what I've said." When we don't specify which thoughts we would like to receive, the other person may respond at great length with thoughts that aren't the ones we are seeking.

- Sometimes we'd like to know whether the person is willing to take certain actions that we've recommended. Such a request may sound like this: "I'd like you to tell me if you would be willing to postpone our meeting for one week."

> (c) whether the listener would be willing to take a particular action.

The use of NVC requires that we be conscious of the specific form of honesty we would like to receive, and to make that request for honesty in concrete language.

Making Requests Of A Group

It is especially important when we are addressing a group to be clear about the kind of understanding or honesty we want back from them after we've expressed ourselves. When we are not clear about the response we'd like, we may initiate unproductive conversations that end up satisfying no one's needs.

I've been invited from time to time to work with groups of citizens concerned about racism in their communities. One issue that frequently arises among these groups is that their meetings are tedious and fruitless. This lack of productivity is very costly for the members, who often expend limited resources to arrange for transportation and childcare in order to attend meetings. Frustrated by prolonged discussions that yield little direction, many members quit the groups, declaring meetings a waste of time. Furthermore, the institutional changes they are striving to make are not usually ones that occur quickly or easily. For all these reasons, when such groups do meet, it's important that they make good use of their time together.

I knew members of one such group that had been organized to effect change in the local school system. It was their belief that various elements in the school system discriminated against students on the basis of race. Because their meetings were unproductive and the group was losing members, they invited me to observe their discussions. I suggested that they conduct their meeting as usual, and that I would let them know if I saw any ways NVC might help.

One man began the meeting by calling the group's attention to a recent newspaper article in which a minority mother had raised complaints and concerns regarding the principal's treatment of her daughter. A woman responded by sharing a situation that had occurred to her when she was a student at the same school. One by one, each member then related a similar personal experience. After twenty minutes I asked the group if their needs were being met by the current discussion. Not one person said "yes." "This is what happens all the time in these meetings!" huffed one man, "I have better things to do with my time than sit around listening to the same old bullshit."

I then addressed the man who had initiated the discussion: "Can you tell me, when you brought up the newspaper article, what response you were wanting from the group?" "I thought it was interesting," he replied. I explained that I was asking what response he wanted from the group, rather than what he thought about the article. He pondered awhile and then conceded, "I'm not sure what I wanted."

> In a group, much time is wasted when speakers aren't certain what response they're wanting back.

And that's why, I believe, twenty minutes of the group's valuable time had been squandered on fruitless discourse. When we address a group without being clear what we are wanting back, unproductive discussions will often follow. However, if even one member of a group is conscious of the importance of clearly requesting the response that is desired, he or she can extend this consciousness to the group. For example, when this particular man didn't define what response he wanted, a member of the group might have said, "I'm confused about how you'd like us to respond to your story. Would you be willing to say what response you'd like from us?" Such interventions can prevent the waste of precious group time.

Conversations often drag on and on, fulfilling no one's needs, because it is unclear whether the initiator of the conversation has gotten what she or he wanted. In India, when people have received the response they want in conversations they have initiated, they say "bas" (pronounced bus). This means, "You need not say more. I feel satisfied and am now ready to move on to something else."

Though we lack such a word in our own language, we can benefit from developing and promoting "bas-consciousness" in all our interactions.

Requests Versus Demands

Requests are received as demands when others believe they will be blamed or punished if they do not comply. When people hear us make a demand, they see only two options: submission or rebellion. Either way, the person requesting is perceived as coercive, and the listener's capacity to respond compassionately to the request is diminished.

> When the other person hears a demand from us, they see two options: submit or rebel.

The more we have in the past blamed, punished, or "laid guilt trips" on others when they haven't responded to our requests, the higher the likelihood that our requests will now be heard as demands. We also pay for the use of such tactics by others. To the degree that people in our lives have been blamed, punished, or urged to feel guilty for not doing what others have requested, the more likely they are to carry this baggage to every subsequent relationship and hear a demand in any request.

> How to tell if it's a demand or a request: Observe what the speaker does if the request is not complied with.

Let's look at two variations of a situation. Jack says to his friend Jane, "I'm lonely and would like you to spend the evening with me." Is that a request or a demand? The answer is that we don't know until we observe how Jack treats Jane if she doesn't comply. Suppose she replies, "Jack, I'm really tired. If you'd like some company, how about finding someone else to be with you this evening?" If Jack then remarks, "How typical of you to be so selfish!" his request was in fact a demand. Instead of empathizing with her need to rest, he has blamed her.

> It's a demand if the speaker then criticizes or judges.

Consider a second scenario:

Jack: "I'm lonely and would like you to spend the evening with me."

Jane: "Jack, I'm really tired. If you'd like some company, how about finding someone else to be with you tonight?"

Jack turns away wordlessly.

Jane, sensing he is upset: "Is something bothering you?"

Jack: "No."

Jane: "Come on, Jack, I can sense something's going on. What's the matter?"

Jack: "You know how lonely I'm feeling. If you really loved me, you'd spend the evening with me."

> **It's a demand if the speaker then lays a guilt-trip.**

Again, instead of empathizing, Jack now interprets Jane's response to mean that she doesn't love him and that she has rejected him.

The more we interpret noncompliance as rejection, the more likely our requests will be heard as demands. This leads to a self-fulfilling prophecy, for the more people hear demands, the less they enjoy being around us.

On the other hand, we would know that Jack's request had been a genuine request, not a demand, if his response to Jane had expressed a respectful recognition of her feelings and needs, e.g. "So, Jane, you're feeling worn out and needing some rest this evening?"

We can help others trust that we are requesting, not demanding, by indicating that we would only want the person to comply if he or she can do so willingly. Thus we might ask, "Would you be willing to set the table?" rather than "I would like you to set the table." However, the most powerful way to

> **It's a request if the speaker then shows empathy toward the other person's needs.**

communicate that we are making a genuine request is to empathize with people when they don't respond to the request. We demonstrate that we are making a request rather than a demand by how we respond when others don't comply. If we are prepared to show an empathic understanding of what prevents someone from doing as we asked, then by my definition, we have made a request, not a demand. Choosing to request rather than demand does not mean we give up when someone says "no" to our request. It does mean that we don't engage in persuasion until we have empathized with what's preventing the other person from saying "yes."

Defining Our Objective When Making Requests

Expressing genuine requests also requires an awareness of our objective. If our objective is only to change people and their behavior or to get our way, then NVC is not an appropriate tool. The process is designed for those of us who would like others to change and respond, but only if they choose to do so willingly and compassionately. The objective of NVC is to establish a relationship based on honesty and empathy. When others trust that our primary commitment is to the quality of the relationship, and that we expect this process to fulfill everyone's needs, then they can trust that our requests are true requests and not camouflaged demands.

> Our objective is a relationship based on honesty and empathy.

A consciousness of this objective is difficult to maintain, especially for parents, teachers, managers, and others whose work centers around influencing people and obtaining behavioral results. A mother who once returned to a workshop after lunch break announced, "Marshall, I went home and tried it. It didn't work." I asked her to describe what she'd done.

"I went home and expressed my feelings and needs, just as we'd practiced. I made no criticism, no judgments of my son. I simply said, 'Look, when I see that you haven't done the work you said you were going to do, I feel very disappointed. I wanted to be able to come home and find the house in order and your chores completed.' Then I made a request: I told him I wanted him to clean it up immediately."

"It sounds like you clearly expressed all the components," I commented, "What happened?"

"He didn't do it."

"Then what happened?" I asked.

"I told him he couldn't go through life being lazy and irresponsible."

I could see that this woman was not yet able to distinguish between expressing requests and making demands. She was still defining the process as successful only if she got compliance for her "requests." During the initial phases of learning this process, we may find ourselves applying the components of NVC mechanically without awareness of the underlying purpose.

Sometimes, however, even when we're conscious of our intent and express our request with care, some people may still hear a demand. This is particularly true when we occupy positions of authority and are speaking with those who have had past experiences with coercive authority figures.

Once, the administrator of a high school invited me to demonstrate to teachers how NVC might be helpful in communicating with students who weren't cooperating as the teachers would have liked.

I was asked to meet with forty students who had been deemed "socially and emotionally maladjusted." I was struck by the way such labels serve as self-fulfilling prophecies. If you were a student who had been thus labeled, wouldn't it just give you permission to have some fun at school by resisting whatever was asked of you? By giving people labels, we tend to act toward them in a way that contributes to the very behavior that concerns us, which we then view as further confirmation of our diagnosis. Since these students knew they had been classified as "socially and emotionally maladjusted," I wasn't surprised that, when I walked in, most of them were hanging out the window hollering obscenities at their friends in the courtyard below. I began by making a request: "I'd like you all to come over and sit down so I can tell you who I am and what I'd like us to do today." About half the students came over. Uncertain that they had all heard me, I repeated my request. With that, the remainder of the students sat down, with the exception of two young men who remained draped over the windowsill.

Unfortunately for me, these two were the biggest students in the class.

"Excuse me," I addressed them, "would one of you two gentlemen tell me what you heard me say?" One of them turned toward me and snorted, "Yeah, you said we had to go over there and sit down." I thought to myself, "Uh, oh, he's heard my request as a demand."

Out loud I said, "Sir" (I've learned always to say "sir" to people with biceps like his, especially when one of them sports a tattoo), "would you be willing to tell me how I could have let you know what I was wanting so that it wouldn't sound like I was bossing you around?" "Huh?" Having been conditioned to expect demands from authorities, he was not used to my different approach. "How can I let you know what I'm wanting from you so it doesn't sound like I don't care about what you'd like?" I repeated. He hesitated for a moment and shrugged, "I don't know."

"What's going on between you and me right now is a good example of what I was wanting us to talk about today. I believe people can enjoy each other a lot better if they can say what they would like without bossing others around. When I tell you what I'd like, I'm not saying that you have to do it or I'll try to make your life miserable. I don't know how to say that in a way that you can trust." To my relief, this seemed to make sense to the young man who, together with his friend, sauntered over to join the group. In certain situations such as this one, it may take awhile for our requests to be clearly seen for what they are.

When making a request, it is also helpful to scan our minds for thoughts of the following sort that automatically transform requests into demands:

- He *should* be cleaning up after himself.
- She's *supposed* to do what I ask.
- I *deserve* to get a raise.
- I'm *justified* in having them stay later.
- I have a *right* to more time off.

When we frame our needs in this way, we are bound to judge others when they don't do as we request. I had such self-righteous thoughts in my mind once when my younger son was not taking out the garbage. When we were dividing the household chores, he had agreed to this task, but every day we would have another struggle about getting the garbage out. Every day I would remind him—"This is your job," "We all have jobs," etc.—with the sole objective of getting him to take out the garbage.

Finally, one night I listened more closely to what he'd been telling me all along about why the garbage wasn't going out. I wrote the following song after that evening's discussion. After my son felt my empathy for his position, he began taking out the garbage without any further reminder from me.

Song from Brett

If I clearly understand
you intend no demand,
I'll usually respond when you call.
But if you come across
like a high and mighty boss,
you'll feel like you ran into a wall.
And when you remind me
so piously
about all those things you've done for me,
you'd better get ready:
Here comes another bout!
Then you can shout,
you can spit,
moan, groan, and throw a fit;
I still won't take the garbage out.
Now even if you should change your style,
It's going to take me a little while
before I can forgive and forget.
Because it seems to me that you
didn't see me as human too
until all your standards were met.

Summary

The fourth component of NVC addresses the question of *what we would like to request of each other to enrich each of our lives.* We try to avoid vague, abstract, or ambiguous phrasing, and remember to use positive action language by stating what we *are* requesting rather than what we are *not.*

When we speak, the clearer we are about what we want back, the more likely we are to get it. Since the message we send is not always the message that's received, we need to learn how to find out if our message has been accurately heard. Especially when we are expressing ourselves in a group, we need to be clear about the nature of the response we are wanting back. Otherwise we may be initiating unproductive conversations that waste considerable group time.

Requests are received as demands when listeners believe that they will be blamed or punished if they do not comply. We can help others trust that we are requesting, not demanding, by indicating our desire for them to comply only if they can do so willingly. The objective of NVC is not to change people and their behavior in order to get our way; it is to establish relationships based on honesty and empathy that will eventually fulfill everyone's needs.

NVC in Action

Sharing Fears About A Best Friend's Smoking

Al and Burt have been best friends for over thirty years. Al, a non-smoker, has done everything he can over the years to persuade Burt to give up his two-pack-a-day habit. Aware during the past year of the increasing severity of his friend's hacking cough, Al finds himself bursting out one day with all the energy and life that had been buried in his unexpressed anger and fear.

Al: Burt, I know we've talked about this a dozen times, but listen. I'm scared your damned cigarettes are going to kill you! You're my best friend, and I want you around for as long as I can have you. Please don't think I'm judging you. I'm not—I'm just really worried. *(In the past, when Al had tried to get him to quit, Burt had often accused Al of judging him.)*

Burt: No, I hear your concern. We've been friends for a long time . . .

Al: *(making a request)* Would you be willing to quit?

Burt: I wish I could.

Al: *(listening for the feelings and needs preventing Burt from agreeing to the request)* Are you scared to try because you don't want to fail?

Burt: Yeah . . . you know how many times I've tried before . . . I know people think less of me for not being able to quit.

Al: *(guessing at what Burt might want to request)* I don't think less of you. And if you tried and failed again, I still wouldn't. I just wish you'd try.

Burt: Thanks. But you're not the only one. . . . It's everyone: you can see it in their eyes—they think you're a failure.

Al: *(empathizing with Burt's feeling)* Is it kind of overwhelming to worry about what others might think, when just quitting is hard enough?

Burt: I really hate the idea that I might be addicted, that I have something that I just can't control . . .

Al: *(his eyes connecting with Burt's, nods head in affirmative. Al's interest and attention to Burt's deep feelings and needs are revealed through his eyes and the silence that follows).*

Burt: I mean, I don't even like smoking any more. It's like you're a pariah if you do it in public. It's embarrassing.

Al: *(continuing to empathize)* It sounds like you'd really like to quit, but are scared you might fail—and how that would be for your self-image and confidence.

Burt: Yeah, I guess that's it. . . . You know, I don't think I've ever talked about it before. Usually when people tell me to quit, I just tell them to get lost. I'd like to quit, but I don't want all that pressure from people.

Al: I wouldn't want to pressure you. I don't know if I could reassure you about your fears around not succeeding, but I sure would like to support you in any way I can. That is . . . if you want me to . . .

Burt: Yes, I do. I'm really touched by your concern and willingness. But . . . suppose I'm not ready to try yet, is that okay with you too?

Al: Of course, Burt, I'll still like you as much. It's just that I want to like you for longer! *(Because Al's request was a genuine request, not a demand, he maintains awareness of his commitment to the quality of the relationship, regardless of Burt's response. He expresses this awareness and his respect for Burt's need for autonomy through the words, "I'll still like you," while simultaneously expressing his own need "to like you for longer.")*

Burt: Well, then, maybe I will try again . . . but don't tell anyone else, okay?

Al: Sure, you decide when you're ready; I won't be mentioning it to anybody.

Exercise 4
EXPRESSING REQUESTS

To see whether we're in agreement about the clear expression of requests, circle the number in front of any of the following statements in which the speaker is clearly requesting that a specific action be taken.

1. "I want you to understand me."

2. "I'd like you to tell me one thing that I did that you appreciate."

3. "I'd like you to feel more confidence in yourself."

4. "I want you to stop drinking."

5. "I'd like you to let me be me."

6. "I'd like you to be honest with me about yesterday's meeting."

7. "I would like you to drive at or below the speed limit."

8. "I'd like to get to know you better."

9. "I would like you to show respect for my privacy."

10. "I'd like you to prepare supper more often."

Here are my responses for Exercise 4:

1. If you circled this number, we're not in agreement. To me, the word "understand" does not clearly express a specific action being requested. Instead, the speaker might have said, "I want you to tell me what you heard me say."

2. If you circled this number, we're in agreement that the statement clearly expresses what the speaker is requesting.

3. If you circled this number, we're not in agreement. To me, the words "feel more confidence" do not clearly express a specific action being requested. The speaker might have said, "I'd like you to take a course in assertiveness training, which I believe would increase your self-confidence."

4. If you circled this number, we're not in agreement. To me, the words "stop drinking" do not clearly express what the speaker wants, but rather what he or she doesn't want. The speaker might have said, "I want you to tell me what needs of yours are met by drinking, and to discuss with me other ways of meeting those needs."

5. If you circled this number, we're not in agreement. To me, the words "let me be me" do not clearly express a specific action being requested. The speaker might have said, "I want you to tell me you won't leave our relationship—even if I do some things that you don't like."

6. If you circled this number, we're not in agreement. To me, the words "be honest with me" do not clearly express a specific action that is being requested. The speaker might have said, "I want you to tell me how you feel about what I did and what you'd like me to do differently."

7. If you circled this number, we're in agreement that the statement clearly expresses what the speaker is requesting.

8. If you circled this number, we're not in agreement. To me, this sentence does not clearly express a specific action being requested. The speaker might have said, "I'd like you to tell me if you would be willing to meet for lunch once a week."

9. If you circled this number, we're not in agreement. To me, the words "show respect for my privacy" do not clearly express a specific action being requested. The speaker might have said, "I'd like you to agree to knock before you enter my office."

10. If you circled this number, we're not in agreement. To me, the words "more often" do not clearly express a specific action being requested. The speaker might have said, "I'd like you to prepare supper every Monday night."

CHAPTER SEVEN

Receiving Empathically

The last four chapters describe the four components of NVC: what we are observing, feeling, and needing, and what we wish to request to enrich our lives. Now we turn from self-expression to apply these same four components to hearing what others are observing, feeling, needing, and requesting. We refer to this part of the communication process as "receiving empathically."

> The two parts of NVC:
> —expressing honestly
> —receiving empathically

Presence: Don't Just Do Something, Stand There

Empathy is a respectful understanding of what others are experiencing. The Chinese philosopher Chuang-Tzu stated that true empathy requires listening with the whole being: "The hearing that is only in the ears is one thing. The hearing of the understanding is another. But the hearing of the spirit is not limited to any one faculty, to the ear, or to the mind. Hence it demands the emptiness of all the faculties. And when the faculties are empty, then the whole being listens. There is then a direct grasp of what is right there before you that can never be heard with the ear or understood with the mind."

> Empathy: emptying the mind and listening with our whole being

In relating to others, empathy occurs only when we have successfully shed all preconceived ideas and judgments about them. The Austrian-born Israeli philosopher Martin Buber describes this quality of presence that life demands of us: "In spite of all similarities, every living situation has, like a newborn child, a new face, that has never been before and will never come again. It demands of you a reaction that cannot be prepared beforehand. It demands nothing of what is past. It demands presence, responsibility; it demands you."

The presence that empathy requires is not easy to maintain. "The capacity to give one's attention to a sufferer is a very rare and difficult thing; it is almost a miracle; it is a miracle," asserts French writer Simone Weil. "Nearly all those who think they have the capacity do not possess it." Instead of empathy, we tend instead to have a strong urge to give advice or reassurance and to explain our own position or feeling. Empathy, on the other hand, requires focusing full attention on the other person's message. We give to others the time and space they need to express themselves fully and to feel understood. There is a Buddhist saying that aptly describes this ability: "Don't just do something, stand there."

> Ask before offering advice or reassurance.

It is often frustrating for someone needing empathy to have us assume that they want reassurance or "fix-it" advice. I received a lesson from my daughter that taught me to check whether advice or reassurance is wanted before offering any. She was looking in the mirror one day and said, "I'm as ugly as a pig."

"You're the most gorgeous creature God ever put on the face of the earth," I declared. She shot me a look of exasperation, exclaimed "Oh, Daddy!", and slammed the door as she left the room. I later found out that she was wanting some empathy. Instead of my ill-timed reassurance, I could have asked, "Are you feeling disappointed with your appearance today?"

My friend Holley Humphrey identified some common behaviors that prevent us from being sufficiently present to connect empathically with others. The following are examples of such obstacles:

- Advising: "I think you should . . . " "How come you didn't . . . ?"
- One-upping: "That's nothing; wait'll you hear what happened to me."
- Educating: "This could turn into a very positive experience for you if you just . . . "

- Consoling: "It wasn't your fault; you did the best you could."
- Story-telling: "That reminds me of the time . . . "
- Shutting down: "Cheer up. Don't feel so bad."
- Sympathizing: "Oh, you poor thing . . . "
- Interrogating: "When did this begin?"
- Explaining: "I would have called but . . . "
- Correcting: "That's not how it happened."

In his book, *When Bad Things Happen to Good People*, Rabbi Harold Kushner describes how painful it was for him, when his son was dying, to hear the words people offered that were intended to make him feel better. Even more painful was his recognition that for twenty years he had been saying the same things to other people in similar situations!

Believing we have to "fix" situations and make others feel better prevents us from being present. Those of us in the role of counselor or psychotherapist are particularly susceptible to this belief. Once, when I was working with twenty-three mental health professionals, I asked them to write, word for word, how they would respond to a client who says, "I'm feeling very depressed. I just don't see any reason to go on." I collected the answers they had written down and announced, "I am now going to read out loud what each of you wrote. Imagine yourself in the role of the person who expressed the feeling of depression, and raise your hand after each statement you hear that gives you a sense that you've been understood." Hands were raised to only three of the twenty-three responses. Questions such as, "When did this begin?" constituted the most frequent response; they give the appearance that the professional is obtaining the information necessary to diagnose and then treat the problem. In fact, such intellectual understanding of a problem blocks the kind of

> Intellectual understanding blocks empathy.

presence that empathy requires. When we are thinking about people's words, listening to how they connect to our theories, we are looking at people—we are not with them. The key ingredient of empathy is presence: we are wholly present with the other party and what they are experiencing. This quality of presence distinguishes empathy from either mental understanding or sympathy. While we may choose at times to sympathize with others by feeling their feelings, it's helpful to be aware that during the moment we are offering sympathy, we are not empathizing.

Listening For Feelings And Needs

In NVC, no matter what words people use to express themselves, we listen for their observations, feelings, and needs, and what they are requesting to enrich life. Imagine having loaned your car to a new neighbor who had approached you with a personal emergency. When your family finds out, they react with intensity, "You are a fool for having trusted a total stranger!" The dialog on the next page shows how to tune in to the feelings and needs of the family members in contrast to either (1) blaming yourself by taking the message personally, or (2) blaming and judging them.

> No matter what others say, we only hear what they are (a) observing, (b) feeling, (c) needing, and (d) requesting.

In this situation, it's obvious what the family is observing and reacting to: the lending of the car to a relative stranger. In other situations, it may not be so clear. If a colleague tells us, "You're not a good team player," we may not know what he or she is observing, although we can usually guess at the behavior that might have triggered such a statement.

The following exchange from a workshop demonstrates the difficulty of focusing on other people's feelings and needs when we are accustomed to assuming responsibility for their feelings and to taking messages personally. The woman in this dialogue wanted to learn to hear the feelings and needs behind certain of her husband's statements. I suggested that she guess at his feelings and needs and then check it out with him.

Husband's statement: "What good does talking to you do? You never listen."

Woman: "Are you feeling unhappy with me?"

MBR: "When you say 'with me,' you imply that his feelings are the result of what you did. I would prefer for you to say, 'Are you unhappy because you were needing . . . ?' and not 'Are you unhappy with me?' It would put your attention on what's going on within him and decrease the likelihood of your taking the message personally."

Woman: "But what would I say? 'Are you unhappy because you . . . ?' Because you what?"

MBR: "Get your clue from the content of your husband's message, 'What good does talking to you do? You never listen.' What is he needing that he's not getting when he says that?"

Woman: *(trying to empathize with the needs being expressed through her husband's message)* "Are you feeling unhappy because you feel like I don't understand you?"

MBR: "Notice that you are focusing on what he's thinking and not what he's needing. I think you'll find people to be less threatening if you hear what they're needing rather than what they're thinking about you. Instead of hearing that he's unhappy because he thinks you don't listen, focus on what he's needing by saying, 'Are you unhappy because you are needing . . .'"

> Listen to what people are needing rather than what they are thinking about us.

Woman: *(trying again)* "Are you feeling unhappy because you are needing to be heard?"

MBR: "That's what I had in mind. Does it make a difference for you to hear him this way?"

Woman: "Definitely—a big difference. I see what's going on for him without hearing that I had done anything wrong."

Paraphrasing

After we focus our attention and hear what others are observing, feeling, and needing and what they are requesting to enrich their lives, we may wish to reflect back by paraphrasing what we have understood. In our previous discussion on requests (Chapter 6), we discussed how to ask for a reflection; now we will look at how to offer it to others.

If we have accurately received the other party's message, our paraphrasing will confirm this for them. If, on the other hand, our paraphrase is incorrect, the speaker has an opportunity to correct us. Another advantage of our choosing to reflect a message back to the other party is that it offers them time to reflect on what they've said and an opportunity to delve deeper into themselves.

NVC suggests that our paraphrasing take the form of questions that reveal our understanding while eliciting any necessary corrections from the speaker. Questions may focus on:

A) what others are observing: "Are you reacting to how many evenings I was gone last week?"

B) how others are feeling and the needs generating their feelings: "Are you feeling hurt because you would have liked more appreciation of your efforts than you received?"

C) what others are requesting: "Are you wanting me to tell you my reasons for saying what I did?"

These questions require us to sense what's going on within other people, while inviting their corrections should we have sensed incorrectly. Notice the difference between these questions and the ones below:

a) "What did I do that you are referring to?"

b) "How are you feeling?" "Why are you feeling that way?"

c) "What are you wanting me to do about it?"

This second set of questions asks for information without first sensing the speaker's reality. Though they may appear to be the most direct way to connect with what's going on within the other person, I've found that questions like these are not the safest route to obtain the information we seek. Many such questions may give speakers the impression that we're a schoolteacher examining

> When asking for information, first express our own feelings and needs.

them or a psychotherapist working on a case. If we do decide to ask for information in this way, however, I've found that people feel safer if we first reveal the feelings and needs within ourselves that are generating the question. Thus, instead of asking someone "What did I do?" we might say, "I'm frustrated because I'd like to be clearer about what you are referring to. Would you be willing to tell me what I've done that leads you to see me in this way?" While this step may not be necessary—or even helpful—in situations where our feelings and needs are clearly conveyed by the context or tone of voice, I would recommend it particularly during moments when the questions we ask are accompanied by strong emotions.

How do we determine if an occasion calls for us to reflect people's messages back to them? Certainly if we are unsure that we have accurately understood the message, we might use paraphrasing to elicit a correction to our guess. But even if we are confident that we've understood them, we may sense the other party wanting confirmation that their message has been accurately received. They may even express this desire overtly by asking, "Is that clear?" or "Do you understand what I mean?" At such moments, hearing a clear paraphrase will often be more reassuring to the speaker than hearing simply, "Yes, I understand."

For example, shortly after participating in an NVC training, a woman volunteer at a hospital was requested by some nurses to talk to an elderly patient: "We've told this woman she isn't that sick and that she'd get better if she took her medicine, but all she does is sit in her room all day long repeating, 'I want to die. I want to die.'" The volunteer approached the elderly woman, and as the nurses had predicted, found her sitting alone, whispering over and over, "I want to die."

"So you would like to die," the volunteer empathized. Surprised, the woman broke off her chant and appeared relieved. She began to talk about how no one understood how terrible she was feeling. The volunteer continued to reflect back the woman's feelings; before long, such warmth had entered their dialogue that they were sitting arms locked around each other. Later that day, the nurses questioned the volunteer about her magic formula: the elderly woman had started to eat and take her medicine, and was apparently in better spirits. Although the nurses had tried to help her with advice and reassurance, it wasn't until her interaction with the volunteer that this woman received what she was truly needing: connection with another human being who could hear her profound despair.

There are no infallible guidelines regarding when to paraphrase, but as a rule of thumb, it is safe to assume that speakers expressing intensely emotional messages would appreciate our reflecting these back to them. When we ourselves are talking, we can make it easier for the listener if we clearly signify when we want or don't want our words to be reflected back to us.

> **Reflect back messages that are emotionally charged.**

There are occasions when we may choose not to verbally reflect someone's statements out of respect for certain cultural norms. For example, a Chinese man once attended a workshop to learn how to hear the feelings and needs behind his father's remarks. Because he could not bear the criticism and attack he continually heard in his father's words, this man dreaded visiting his father and avoided him for months at a time. He came to me ten years later and reported that his ability to hear feelings and needs had radically transformed his relationship with his father to the point where they now enjoy a close and loving connection. Although he listens for his father's feelings and needs, however, he does not paraphrase

> **Paraphrase only when it contributes to greater compassion and understanding.**

what he hears. "I never say it out loud." he explained, "In our culture, to direct-talk to a person about their feelings is something they're not used to. But thanks to the fact that I no longer hear what he says as an attack, but as his own feelings and needs, our relationship has become enormously wonderful."

"So you're never going to talk directly to him about feelings, but it helps to be able to hear them?" I asked.

"No, now I think I'm probably ready," he answered. "Now that we have such a solid relationship, if I were to say to him, 'Dad, I'd like to be able to talk directly to you about what we are feeling,' I think he just might be ready to do it."

When we paraphrase, the tone of voice we use is highly important. When they hear themselves reflected back, people are likely to be sensitive to the slightest hint of criticism or sarcasm. They are likewise negatively affected by a declarative tone that implies that we are telling them what is going on inside of them. If we are consciously listening for other people's feelings and needs, however, our tone communicates that we're asking whether we have understood—not claiming that we have understood.

We also need to be prepared for the possibility that the intention behind our paraphrasing will be misinterpreted. "Don't pull any of that psychology crap on me!" we may be told. Should this occur, we continue our effort to sense the speaker's feelings and needs; perhaps we see in this case that the speaker doesn't trust our motives and needs more understanding of our intentions before he can appreciate hearing our paraphrases. As we've seen, all criticism, attack, insults, and judgments vanish when we focus attention on hearing the feelings and needs behind a message. The more we practice in this way, the more we realize a simple truth: behind all those messages we've allowed ourselves to be intimidated by are just individuals with unmet needs appealing to us to contribute to their well-being. When we receive messages with this awareness, we never feel dehumanized by what others

> Behind intimidating messages are simply people appealing to us to meet their needs.

> A difficult message becomes an opportunity to enrich someone's life.

have to say to us. We only feel dehumanized when we get trapped in derogatory images of other people or thoughts of wrongness about ourselves. As author and mythologist Joseph Campbell suggested, "'What will they think of me?' must be put aside for bliss." We begin to feel this bliss when messages previously experienced as critical or blaming begin to be seen for the gifts they are: opportunities to give to people who are in pain.

If it happens regularly that people distrust our motives and sincerity when we paraphrase their words, we may need to examine our own intentions more closely. Perhaps we are paraphrasing and engaging the components of NVC in a mechanistic way without maintaining clear consciousness of purpose. We might ask ourselves, for example, whether we are more intent on applying the process "correctly" than on connecting with the human being in front of us. Or perhaps, even though we are using the form of NVC, our only interest is in changing the other person's behavior.

Some people resist paraphrasing as a waste of time. One city administrator explained during a practice session, "I'm paid to give facts and solutions, not to sit around doing psychotherapy with everyone who comes into my office." This same administrator, however, was being confronted by angry citizens who would come to him with their passionate concerns and leave dissatisfied for not having been heard. Some of these citizens later confided to me, "When you go to his office, he gives you a bunch of facts, but you

> Paraphrasing saves time.

never know whether he's heard you first. When that happens, you start to distrust his facts." Paraphrasing tends to save, rather than waste, time. Studies in labor-management negotiations demonstrate that the time required to reach conflict resolution is cut in half when each negotiator agrees, before responding, to accurately repeat what the previous speaker had said.

I recall a man who was initially skeptical about the value of paraphrasing. He and his wife were attending an NVC workshop during a time when their marriage was beset by serious problems. During the workshop, his wife said to him, "You never listen to me."

"I do too," he replied.

"No, you don't," she countered.

I addressed the husband: "I'm afraid you just proved her point. You didn't respond in a way that lets her know that you were listening to her."

He was puzzled by the point I was making, so I asked for permission to play his role—which he gladly gave since he wasn't having too much success with it. His wife and I then had the following exchange:

Wife: "You never listen to me."

MBR in role of husband: "It sounds like you're terribly frustrated because you would like to feel more connection when we speak."

The wife was moved to tears when she finally received this confirmation that she had been understood. I turned to the husband and explained, "I believe this is what she is telling you she needs—a reflection of her feelings and needs as a confirmation that she'd been heard." The husband seemed dumfounded. "Is that all she wanted?" he asked, incredulous that such a simple act could have had such a strong impact on his wife.

A short time later, he enjoyed the satisfaction firsthand when his wife reflected back to him a statement that he had made with great emotional intensity. Savoring her paraphrase, he looked at me and declared, "It's valid." It is a poignant experience to receive concrete evidence that someone is empathically connected to us.

Sustaining Empathy

I recommend allowing others the opportunity to fully express themselves before turning our attention to solutions or requests for relief. When we proceed too quickly to what people might be requesting, we may not convey our genuine interest in their feelings and needs; instead, they may get the impression that we're in a hurry to either be free of them or to fix their problem. Furthermore, an initial message is often like the tip of an iceberg;

it may be followed by yet unexpressed, but related—and often more powerful—feelings. By maintaining our attention on what's going on within others, we offer them a chance to fully explore and express their interior selves. We would stem this flow if we were to shift attention too quickly either to their request or to our own desire to express ourselves.

> **Staying with empathy, we allow speakers to touch deeper levels of themselves.**

Suppose a mother comes to us, saying, "My child is impossible. No matter what I tell him to do, he doesn't listen." We might reflect her feelings and needs by saying, "It sounds like you're feeling desperate and would like to find some way of connecting with your son." Such a paraphrase often encourages a person to look within. If we have accurately reflected her statement, the mother might touch upon other feelings: "Maybe it's my fault. I'm always yelling at him." As the listener, we would continue to stay with the feelings and needs being expressed and say, for example, "Are you feeling guilty because you would have liked to have been more understanding of him than you have been at times?" If the mother continues to sense understanding in our reflection, she might move further into her feelings and declare, "I'm just a failure as a mother." We continue to remain with the feelings and needs being expressed: "So you're feeling discouraged and want to relate differently to him?" We persist in this manner until the person has exhausted all her feelings surrounding this issue.

> **We know the speaker has received adequate empathy when a. we sense a release of tension, or b. the flow of words comes to a halt.**

What evidence is there that we've adequately empathized with the other person? First, when an individual realizes that everything going on within has received full empathic understanding, they will experience a sense of relief. We can become aware of this phenomenon by noticing a corresponding release of tension in our own body. A second even more obvious sign is that the person will stop talking. If we are uncertain as to whether we have stayed long enough in the process, we can always ask, "Is there more that you wanted to say?"

When Pain Blocks Our Ability To Empathize

It is impossible for us to give something to another if we don't have it ourselves. Likewise, if we find ourselves unable or unwilling to empathize despite our efforts, it is usually a sign that we are too starved for empathy to be able to offer it to others. Sometimes if we openly acknowledge that our own distress is preventing us from responding empathically, the other person may come through with the empathy we need.

> We need empathy to give empathy.

At other times, it may be necessary to provide ourselves with some "emergency first aid" empathy by listening to what's going on in ourselves with the same quality of presence and attention that we offer to others. The former United Nations secretary-general, Dag Hammarskjold, once said, "The more faithfully you listen to the voice within you, the better you will hear what is happening outside." If we become skilled in giving ourselves empathy, we often experience in just a few seconds a natural release of energy that then enables us to be present with the other person. If this fails to happen, however, we have a couple of other choices.

We can scream—nonviolently. I recall spending three days mediating between two gangs that had been killing each other off. One gang called themselves Black Egyptians; the other, the East St. Louis Police Department. The score was two to one—a total of three dead within a month. After three tense days trying to bring these groups together to hear each other and resolve their differences, I was driving home and thinking how I never wanted to be in the middle of a conflict again for the rest of my life.

The first thing I saw when I walked through the back door was my children entangled in a fight. I had no energy to empathize with them so I screamed nonviolently: "Hey, I'm in a lot of pain! Right now I really do *not* want to deal with your fighting! I just want some peace and quiet!" My older son, then nine, stopped short, looked at me, and asked, "Do you want to talk about it?" If we are able to speak our pain nakedly without blame, I find that even people in distress are sometimes able to hear our need. Of course I wouldn't want to scream, "What's the matter with you? Don't you know how to behave any better? I just got home after a rough day!" or insinuate in any way that their behavior is at fault. I scream nonviolently by calling attention to my own desperate needs and pain in this moment.

If, however, the other party is also experiencing such intensity of feelings that they can neither hear us nor leave us alone, the third recourse is to physically remove ourselves from the situation. We give ourselves time out and the opportunity to acquire the empathy we need to return in a different frame of mind.

Summary

Empathy is a respectful understanding of what others are experiencing. Instead of offering empathy, we often have a strong urge to give advice or reassurance and to explain our own position or feeling. Empathy, however, calls upon us to empty our mind and listen to others with our whole being.

In NVC, no matter what words others may use to express themselves, we simply listen for their observations, feelings, needs, and requests. Then we may wish to reflect back, paraphrasing what we have understood. We stay with empathy, allowing others the opportunity to fully express themselves before we turn our attention to solutions or requests for relief.

We need empathy to give empathy. When we sense ourselves being defensive or unable to empathize, we need to (a) stop, breathe, give ourselves empathy, (b) scream nonviolently, or (c) take time out.

NVC in Action

A Wife Connects With Her Dying Husband

A patient has just been diagnosed with an advanced state of lung cancer. The following scene at his home, involving a visiting nurse, the patient, and his wife, represents a last opportunity for him to connect emotionally with his wife and discuss his dying before being admitted to the hospital. The wife begins the conversation with the nurse by complaining about the physical therapist who was part of the home health care team assigned to her husband's care.

Wife: She's a bad therapist.

Nurse: *(listening empathically to what the wife is feeling and wanting)* Are you feeling annoyed and wanting to see a different quality of care?

Wife: She doesn't do anything. She made him stop walking when his pulse got high.

Nurse: *(continuing to hear the wife's feelings and wants)* Is it because you want your husband to get better that you're scared if the physical therapist doesn't push him, he won't get stronger?

Wife: *(starts to cry)* Yes, I'm so scared!

Nurse: Are you scared of losing him?

Wife: Yes, we've been together so long.

Nurse: *(listening for other feelings behind the fear)* Are you worrying about how you would feel if he dies?

Wife: I just can't imagine how I am going to live without him. He's always been there for me. Always.

Nurse: So you're sad when you think of living without him?

Wife: There is no one else besides him. He's all I have, you know. My daughter won't even talk to me.

Nurse: It sounds like when you think of your daughter, you feel frustrated because you wish you had a different relationship with her.

Wife: I wish I did, but she is such a selfish person. I don't know why I even bothered having kids. A lot of good it does me now!

Nurse: Sounds to me like you might be somewhat angry and disappointed because you want more support from the family during your husband's illness.

Wife: Yes, he's so sick; I don't know how I am going to get through this alone. I haven't anyone . . . not even to talk to, except with you here . . . now. Even he won't talk about it. . . . Look at him! *(Husband remains silent and impassive.)* He doesn't say anything!

Nurse: Are you sad, wishing the two of you could support each other and feel more connected?

Wife: Yes. *(She pauses, then makes a request)* Talk to him the way you talk to me.

Nurse: *(wishing to clearly understand the need that is being addressed behind the wife's request)* Are you wanting him to be listened to in a way that helps him express what he's feeling inside?

Wife: Yes, yes, that's exactly it! I want him to feel comfortable talking and I want to know what he is feeling. *(Using the nurse's guess, the wife is able to first become aware of what she wanted and then find the words to articulate it. This is a key moment: often it is difficult for people to identify what they want in a situation, even though they may know what they don't want. We see how a clear request—"Talk to him the way you talk to me"—is a gift that empowers the other person. The nurse is now able to act in a way she knows to be in harmony with the wife's wishes. This alters the atmosphere in the room, as the nurse and the wife now "work together," both in a compassionate mode.)*

Nurse: *(turning to the husband)* How do you feel when you hear what your wife has shared?

Husband: I really love her.

Nurse: Are you glad to have an opportunity to talk about this with her?

Husband: Yes, we need to talk about it.

Nurse: Would you be willing to say how you are feeling about the cancer?

Husband: *(after a brief silence)* Not very good. *(The words "good" and "bad" are often used to describe feelings when people have yet to identify the specific emotion they are experiencing. Expressing his feelings more precisely would help him with the emotional connection he is seeking with his wife.)*

Nurse: *(encouraging him to move toward more precision)* Are you scared about dying?

Husband: No, not scared. *(Notice the nurse's incorrect guess does not hamper the continued flow of dialogue.)*

Nurse: Do you feel angry about dying? *(Because this patient isn't able to verbalize his internal experience easily, the nurse continues to support him in the process.)*

Husband: No, not angry.

Nurse: *(At this point, after two incorrect guesses, the nurse decides to express her own feelings)* Well, now I'm puzzled about what you may be feeling, and wonder if you can tell me.

Husband: I reckon, I'm thinking how she'll do without me.

Nurse: Oh, are you worried she may not be able to handle her life without you?

Husband: Yes, worried she'll miss me.

Nurse: *(She is aware that dying patients often hang on*

due to worry over those they are leaving behind. Patients sometimes need the reassurance that loved ones can accept their death before they can let themselves go.) Do you want to hear how your wife feels when you say that?

Husband: Yes.

Here the wife joins the conversation; in the continued presence of the nurse, the couple begins to express themselves openly to each other. In this dialogue, the wife begins with a complaint about the physical therapist. However, after a series of exchanges during which she felt empathically received, she is able to determine that what she really seeks is a deeper connection with her husband during this critical stage of their lives.

Exercise 5
DIFFERENTIATING RECEIVING EMPATHICALLY FROM RECEIVING NON-EMPATHICALLY.

If you would like an exercise to see whether we are communicating about empathy, please circle the number in front of the statements in which the person B is responding empathically to what is going on within Person A.

1. Person A: How could I do something so stupid?
   Person B: Nobody is perfect; you're too hard on yourself.

2. Person A: If you ask me, we ought to ship all these immigrants back to where they came from.
   Person B: Do you really think that would solve anything?

3. Person A: You aren't God!
   Person B: Are you feeling frustrated because you would like me to admit that there can be other ways of interpreting this matter?

4. Person A: I think that you take me for granted. I wonder how you would manage without me.
   Person B: That's not true! I don't take you for granted.

5. Person A: How could you say a thing like that to me?
   Person B: Are you feeling hurt because I said that?

6. Person A: I'm furious with my husband. He's never around when I need him.
   Person B: You think he should be around more than he is?

7. Person A: I'm disgusted with how heavy I'm getting.
   Person B: Perhaps jogging would help.

8. Person A: I've been a nervous wreck planning for my daughter's wedding. Her fiancé's family is not helping. About every day they change their minds about the kind of wedding they would like.

Person B: So you're feeling nervous about how to make arrangements and would appreciate it if your future in-laws could be more aware of the complications their indecision creates for you?

9. Person A: When my relatives come without letting me know ahead of time I feel invaded. It reminds me of how my parents used to disregard my needs and would plan things for me.
Person B: I know how you feel. I used to feel that way too.

10. Person A: I'm disappointed with your performance. I would have liked your department to double your production last month.
Person B: I understand that you are disappointed, but we have had many absences due to illness.

Here are my responses to Exercise 5:

1. I didn't circle this one because I see Person B giving reassurance rather than empathically receiving what Person A is expressing.

2. I see Person B attempting to educate rather than empathically receiving what Person A is expressing.

3. If you circled this we are in agreement. I see Person B empathically receiving what Person A is expressing.

4. I see Person B disagreeing and defending rather than empathically receiving what is going on in Person A.

5. I see Person B taking responsibility for Person A's feelings rather than empathically receiving what is going on in Person A. Person B might have said, "Are you feeling hurt because you would have liked me to agree to do Is you requested?"

6. If you circled this we are in partial agreement. I see Person B receiving Person A's thoughts. However, I believe we are connected more deeply when we receive the feelings and needs being expressed rather than the thought. Therefore, I would

have preferred it if Person B had said, "So you're feeling furious because you would like him to be around more than he is?"

7. I see Person B giving advice rather than empathically receiving what is going on in Person A.

8. If you circled this we are in agreement. I see Person B empathically receiving what is going on in Person A.

9. I see Person B assuming that he/she has understood and talking about his/her own feelings rather than empathically receiving what is going on in Person A.

10. I see Person B starting by focusing on Person A's feelings but then shifting to explaining.

CHAPTER EIGHT

The Power of Empathy

Empathy That Heals

Carl Rogers described the impact of empathy on its recipients: "When . . . someone really hears you without passing judgment on you, without trying to take responsibility for you, without trying to mold you, it feels damn good. . . . When I have been listened to and when I have been heard, I am able to re-perceive my world in a new way and go on. It is astonishing how elements that seem insoluble become soluble when someone listens. How confusions that seem irremediable turn into relatively clear flowing streams when one is heard."

> Empathy allows us "to reperceive [our] world in a new way and move on."

One of my favorite stories about empathy comes from the principal of an innovative school. She had returned after lunch one day to find Milly, an elementary school student, sitting dejectedly in her office waiting to see her. She sat down next to Milly, who began, "Mrs. Anderson, have you ever had a week when everything you did hurt somebody else, and you never intended to hurt anyone at all?"

"Yes," the principal replied, "I think I understand," whereupon Milly proceeded to describe her week. "By now," the principal related, "I was quite late for a very important meeting—still had my coat on—and anxious not to keep a room full of people waiting, and so I asked, 'Milly, what can I do for you?' Milly reached over, took both my shoulders in her hands, looked me straight in the

> "Don't just do something. . . ."

eyes, and said very firmly, 'Mrs. Anderson, I don't want you to *do* anything; I just want you to listen.'

This was one of the most significant moments of learning in my life—taught to me by a child—so I thought, 'Never mind the roomful of adults waiting for me!' Milly and I moved over to a bench that afforded us more privacy and sat, my arm around her shoulders, her head on my chest, and her arm around my waist, while she talked until she was done. And you know, it didn't take that long."

One of the most satisfying aspects of my work is to hear how individuals have used NVC to strengthen their ability to connect empathically with others. My friend Laurence, who lives in Switzerland, described how upset she had felt when her 6-year-old son had stormed away angrily while she was still talking to him. Isabelle, her 10-year-old daughter who had accompanied her to a recent NVC workshop, remarked, "So you're really angry, Mom. You'd like for him to talk when he's angry and not run off." Laurence marveled at how, upon hearing Isabelle's words, she had felt an immediate diminishing of tension, and was subsequently able to be more understanding with her son when he returned.

A college instructor described how relationships between students and faculty had been affected when several members of the faculty learned to listen empathically and to express themselves more vulnerably and honestly. "The students opened up more and more and told us about the various personal problems that were interfering with their studies. The more they talked about it, the more work they were able to complete. Even though this kind of listening took a lot of our time, we were glad to spend it in this way. Unfortunately, the dean got upset; he said we were not counselors and should spend more time teaching and less time talking with the students."

When I asked how the faculty had dealt with this, the instructor replied, "We empathized with the dean's concern. We heard that he felt worried and wanted to know that we weren't getting involved in things we couldn't handle. We also heard that he needed reassurance that the time spent on talking wasn't cutting into our teaching responsibilities. He seemed relieved by the way we listened to him. We continued to talk with the students because we could see that the more we listened to them, the better they did in their studies."

When we work in a hierarchically structured institution, there is a tendency to hear commands and judgments from those higher up in the hierarchy. While we may easily empathize with our peers and those in less powerful positions, we may find ourselves being defensive or apologetic, instead of empathic, in the presence of those we identify as our "superiors." This is why I was particularly pleased that these faculty members had remembered to empathize with their dean as well as with their students.

> It's harder to empathize with those who appear to possess more power, status, or resources.

Empathy And The Ability To Be Vulnerable

Because we are called to reveal our deepest feelings and needs, we may sometimes find it challenging to express ourselves in NVC. Self-expression becomes easier, however, after we empathize with others because we will then have touched their humanness and realized the common qualities we share. The more we connect with the feelings and needs behind their words, the less frightening it is to open up to other people. The situations where we are the most reluctant to express vulnerability are often those where we want to maintain a "tough image" for fear of losing authority or control.

> The more we empathize with the other party, the safer we feel.

Once I showed my vulnerability to some members of a street gang in Cleveland by acknowledging the hurt I was feeling and my desire to be treated with more respect. "Oh, look," one of them remarked, "he's feeling hurt; isn't that too bad!" at which point all his friends chimed in laughing. Here again, I could interpret them as taking advantage of my vulnerability (Option 2 - "Blame others") or I could empathize with the feelings and needs behind their behavior (Option 4).

If, however, I have an image that I'm being humiliated and taken advantage of, I may be too wounded, angry, or scared to be able to empathize. At such a moment, I would need to withdraw physically in order to offer myself some empathy or to request it from a reliable source. After I have discovered the needs that had been so powerfully triggered in me and have received adequate empathy for them, I shall then be ready to return and empathize with the other party. In situations of pain, I recommend first getting the empathy necessary to go beyond the thoughts occupying our heads so as to recognize our deeper needs.

As I listened closely to the gang member's remark, "Oh look, he's feeling hurt, isn't that too bad?" and the laughter that followed, I sensed that he and his friends were annoyed and not wanting to be subjected to guilt trips and manipulation. They may have been reacting to people in their pasts who used phrases like "that hurts me" to imply disapproval. Since I didn't verify it with them out loud, I have no way of knowing if my guess was in fact accurate. Just focusing my attention there, however, kept me from either taking it personally or getting angry. Instead of judging them for ridiculing or treating me disrespectfully, I concentrated on hearing the pain and needs behind such behavior.

"Hey," one of them burst out, "this is a bunch of crap you're offering us! Suppose there are members of another gang here and they have guns and you don't. And you say just stand there and *talk* to them? Crap!"

Then everybody was laughing again, and again I directed my attention to their feelings and needs: "So it sounds like you're really fed up with learning something that has no relevance in those situations?"

"Yeah, and if you lived in this neighborhood, you'd *know* this is a bunch of crap."

"So you need to trust that someone teaching you something has some knowledge of your neighborhood?"

"Damn right. Some of these dudes would blast you away before you got two words out of your mouth!"

"And you need to trust that someone trying to teach you something understands the dangers around here?" I continued to listen in this manner, sometimes verbalizing what I heard and sometimes not. This continued for forty-five minutes and then I sensed a shift: they felt that I was truly understanding them. A counselor in the program noticed the shift, and asked them out loud, "What do you think of this man?" The gentleman who had been giving me the roughest time replied, "He's the best speaker we've ever had."

Astonished, the counselor turned to me and whispered, "But you haven't said anything!" In fact, I had said a lot by demonstrating that there was nothing they could throw at me that couldn't be translated into universal human feelings and needs.

> We "say a lot" by listening for other people's feelings and needs.

Using Empathy To Defuse Danger

The ability to offer empathy to people in stressful situations can defuse potential violence.

A teacher in the inner city of St. Louis related an incident where she had conscientiously stayed after school to help a student, even though teachers were warned to leave the building for their own safety after classes were dismissed. A stranger entered her classroom, where the following exchange took place:

Young man: "Take off your clothes."

Teacher (noticing that he was shaking): "I'm sensing this is very scary for you."

Young man: "Did you hear me? God damn it, take off your clothes!"

Teacher: "I'm sensing you're really pissed off right now and you want me to do what you're telling me."

Young man: "You're damned right, and you're going to get hurt if you don't."

Teacher: "I'd like you to tell me if there's some other way of meeting your needs that wouldn't hurt me."

Young man: "I said take them off."

Teacher: "I can hear how much you want this. At the same time, I want you to know how scared and horrible I feel, and how grateful I'd be if you'd leave without hurting me."

Young man: "Give me your purse."

The teacher handed the stranger her purse, relieved not to be raped. She later described how, each time she empathized with the young man, she could sense his becoming less adamant in his intention to follow through with the rape.

A metropolitan police officer attending a follow-up training in NVC once greeted me with this account:

> I'm sure glad you had us practicing empathy with angry people that last time. Just a few days after our session, I went to arrest someone in a public housing project. When I brought him out, my car was surrounded by about 60 people screaming things at me like, 'Let him go! He didn't do anything! You police are a bunch of racist pigs!' Although I was skeptical that empathy would help, I didn't have many other options. So I reflected back the feelings that were coming at me; I said things like, 'So you don't trust my reasons for arresting this man? You think it has to do with race?' After several minutes of my continuing to reflect their feelings, the group became less hostile. In the end they opened a path so I could get to my car.

Finally, I'd like to illustrate how a young woman used empathy to bypass violence during her night shift at a drug detoxification center in Toronto. The young woman recounted this story during a second workshop she attended in NVC. At 11:00 p.m. one night, a few weeks after her first NVC training, a man who'd obviously been taking drugs walked in off the street and demanded a room. The young woman started to explain to him that all the rooms had been filled for the night. She was about to hand the man the address of another detox center when he hurled her to the ground. "The next thing I knew, he was sitting across my chest holding a knife to my throat and shouting, 'You bitch, don't lie to me! You do too have a room!'"

She then proceeded to apply her training by listening for his feelings and needs.

"You remembered to do that under those conditions?" I asked, impressed.

"What choice did I have? Desperation sometimes makes good communicators of us all! You know, Marshall," she added, "that joke you told in the workshop really helped me. In fact, I think it saved my life."

"What joke?"

"Remember when you said never to put your 'but' in the face of an angry person? I was all ready to start arguing with him; I was about to say, '*But* I don't have a room!' when I remembered your joke. It had really stayed with me because only the week before, I was arguing with my mother and she'd said to me, 'I could kill you when you answer "but" to everything I say!' Imagine, if my own mother was angry enough to kill me for using that word, what would this man have done? If I'd said, 'But I don't have a room!' when he was screaming at me, I have no doubt he would have slit my throat.

So instead, I took a deep breath and said, 'It sounds like you're really angry and you want to be given a room.' He yelled back, 'I may be an addict, but by God, I deserve respect. I'm tired of nobody giving me respect. My parents don't give me respect. I'm gonna get respect!' I just focused on his feelings and needs and said, 'Are you fed up, not getting the respect that you want?'"

> Empathize, rather than put your "but" in the face of an angry person.

"How long did this go on?" I asked.

"Oh, about another 35 minutes," she replied.

"That must have been terrifying."

"No, not after the first couple of interchanges, because then something else we'd learned here became apparent. When I concentrated on listening for his feelings and needs, I stopped seeing him as a monster. I could see, just as you'd said, how people who seem like monsters are simply human beings whose language and behavior sometimes keep us from seeing their humanness. The more I was able to focus my attention on his

> **When we listen for their feelings and needs, we no longer see people as monsters.**

feelings and needs, the more I saw him as a person full of despair whose needs weren't being met. I became confident that if I held my attention there, I wouldn't be hurt. After he'd received the empathy he needed, he got off me, put the knife away, and I helped him find a room at another center."

Delighted that she'd learned to respond empathically in such an extreme situation, I asked curiously, "What are you doing back here? It sounds like you've mastered NVC and should be out teaching others what you've learned."

"Now I need you to help me with a hard one," she said.

"I'm almost afraid to ask. What could be harder than that?"

"Now I need you to help me with my mother. Despite all the insight I got into that 'but' phenomenon, you know what happened? At supper the next evening when I told my mother what had happened with the man, she said, 'You're going to cause your father and me to have a heart attack if you keep that job. You simply have to

> **It may be difficult to empathize with those who are closest to us.**

find different work!' So guess what I said to her? '*But*, mother, it's my life!'"

I couldn't have asked for a more compelling example of how difficult it can be to respond empathically to one's own family members!

Empathy In Hearing Someone's "No!"

Because of our tendency to read rejection into someone else's "no" and "I don't want to . . . ," these are important messages for us to be able to empathize with. If we take them personally, we may feel hurt without understanding what's actually going on within the other person. When we shine the light of consciousness on

> Empathizing with someone's "no" protects us from taking it personally.

the feelings and needs behind someone else's "no," however, we become cognizant of what they are wanting that prevents them from responding as we would like.

One time I asked a woman during a workshop break to join me and other participants for some ice cream nearby. "No!" she replied brusquely. The tone of her voice led me to interpret her answer as a rejection, until I reminded myself to tune in to the feelings and needs she might be expressing through her "no." "I sense that you are angry," I said. "Is that so?"

"No," she replied, "it's just that I don't want to be corrected every time I open my mouth."

Now I sensed that she was fearful rather than angry. I checked this out by asking, "So you're feeling fearful and want to protect yourself from being in a situation where you might be judged for how you communicate?"

"Yes," she affirmed, "I can imagine sitting in the ice cream shop with you and having you notice everything I say."

I then discovered that the way I'd been providing feedback in the workshop had been frightening to her. My empathy for her message had taken the sting out of her "no" for me: I heard her desire to avoid receiving similar feedback in public. Assuring her that I wouldn't evaluate her communication in public, I then conferred with her on ways to give feedback that would leave her feeling safe. And yes, she joined the group for ice cream.

Empathy To Revive A Lifeless Conversation

We have all found ourselves in the midst of a lifeless conversation. Perhaps we're at a social event, hearing words without feeling any connection to the speaker. Or we're listening to a "Babble-on-ian"—a term coined by my friend Kelly Bryson for someone who elicits in their listeners the fear of interminable conversation. Vitality drains out of conversations when we lose connection with the feelings and needs generating the speaker's words, and with the requests associated with those needs. This is common when people talk without consciousness of what they are feeling, needing, or requesting. Instead of being engaged in an exchange of life energy with other human beings, we see ourselves becoming wastebaskets for their words.

How and when do we interrupt a dead conversation to bring it back to life? I'd suggest the best time to interrupt is when we've heard one word more than we want to hear. The longer we wait, the harder it is to be civil when we do step in. Our intention in interrupting is not to claim the floor for ourselves, but to help the speaker connect to the life energy behind the words being spoken.

We do this by tuning in to possible feelings and needs. Thus, if an aunt is repeating the story about how 20 years ago her husband deserted her with two small children, we might interrupt by saying, "So, Auntie, it sounds like you are still feeling hurt, wishing you'd been treated more fairly."

> To bring a conversation back to life: interrupt with empathy.

People are not aware that it is often empathy they are needing. Neither do they realize that they are more likely to receive that empathy by expressing the feelings and needs that are alive in them rather than by recounting tales of past injustice and hardship.

Another way to bring a conversation to life is to openly express our desire to be more connected, and to request information that would help us establish that connection. Once at a cocktail party I was in the midst of an abundant flow of words that to me, however, seemed lifeless. "Excuse me," I broke in, addressing the group of nine other people I'd found myself with, "I'm feeling impatient because I'd like to be more connected with you, but our conversation isn't creating the kind of connection I'm wanting. I'd like to know if the conversation we've been having is meeting your needs, and if so, what needs of yours were being met through it."

All nine people stared at me as if I had thrown a rat in the punch bowl. Fortunately, I remembered to tune in to the feelings and needs being expressed through their silence. "Are you annoyed with my interrupting because you would have liked to continue the conversation?" I asked.

After another silence, one of the men replied, "No, I'm not annoyed. I was thinking about what you were asking. No, I wasn't enjoying the conversation; in fact, I was totally bored with it."

At the time, I was surprised to hear his response because he had been the one doing most of the talking! Now I am no longer surprised: I have since discovered that conversations that are lifeless for the listener are equally so for the speaker.

> What bores the listener bores the speaker too.

You may wonder how we can muster the courage to flatly interrupt someone in the middle of a sentence. I once conducted an informal survey, posing the following question: "If you are using more words than somebody wants to hear, do you want that person to pretend to listen or to stop you?" Of the scores of people I approached, all but one expressed a preference to be stopped. Their answers gave me courage by convincing me that it is more considerate to interrupt people than to pretend to listen. All of us want our words to enrich others, not to burden them.

> Speakers prefer that listeners interrupt rather than pretend to listen.

Empathy For Silence

One of the hardest messages for many of us to empathize with is silence. This is especially true when we've expressed ourselves vulnerably and need to know how others are reacting to our words. At such times, it's easy to project our worst fears onto the lack of response and forget to connect with the feelings and needs being expressed through the silence.

Once when I was working with the staff of a business organization, I was talking about something deeply emotional and began to cry. When I looked up, I received a response from the organization's director that was not easy for me to receive: silence. He turned his face from me with what I interpreted to be an expression of disgust. Fortunately, I remembered to put my attention on what might be going on within him, and said, "I'm sensing from your response to my crying that you're feeling disgusted, and you'd prefer to have someone more in control of his feelings consulting with your staff."

> Empathize with silence by listening for the feelings and needs behind it.

If he had answered "yes," I would have been able to accept that we had different values around expressing emotions, without somehow thinking that I was wrong for having expressed my emotions as I did. But instead of "yes," the director replied, "No, not at all. I was just thinking of how my wife wishes I could cry." He went on to reveal that his wife, who was divorcing him, had been complaining that living with him was like living with a rock.

During my practice as a psychotherapist, I was once contacted by the parents of a 20-year-old woman under psychiatric care who, for several months, had been undergoing medication, hospitalization, and shock treatments. She had become mute three months before her parents contacted me. When they brought her to my office, she had to be assisted because, left to herself, she didn't move.

In my office, she crouched in her chair, shaking, her eyes on the floor. Trying to connect empathically with the feelings and needs being expressed through her nonverbal message, I said, "I'm sensing that you are frightened and would like to be sure that it's safe to talk. Is that accurate?"

She showed no reaction, so I expressed my own feeling by saying, "I'm very concerned about you, and I'd like you to tell me if there's something I could say or do to make you feel safer." Still no response. For the next forty minutes, I continued to either reflect her feelings and needs or express my own. There was no visible response, nor even the slightest recognition that I was trying to communicate with her. Finally I expressed that I was tired, and that I wanted her to return the following day.

The next few days were like the first. I continued focusing my attention on her feelings and needs, sometimes verbally reflecting what I understood and sometimes doing so silently. From time to time I would express what was going on in myself. She sat shaking in her chair, saying nothing.

On the fourth day, when she still didn't respond, I reached over and held her hand. Not knowing whether my words were communicating my concern, I hoped the physical contact might do so more effectively. At first contact, her muscles tensed and she shrank further back into her chair. I was about to release her hand when I sensed a slight yielding, so I kept my hold; after a few moments I noticed a progressive relaxation on her part. I held her hand for several minutes while I talked to her as I had the first few days. Still she said nothing.

When she arrived the next day, she appeared even more tense than before, but there was one difference: she extended a clenched fist toward me while turning her face away from me. I was at first confused by the gesture, but then sensed she had something in her hand she wanted me to have. Taking her fist in my hand, I pried open her fingers. In her palm was a crumpled note with the following message: "Please help me say what's inside."

I was elated to receive this sign of her desire to communicate. After another hour of encouragement, she finally expressed a first sentence, slowly and fearfully. When I reflected back what I had heard her saying, she appeared relieved and then continued, slowly and fearfully, to talk. A year later, she sent me a copy of the following entries from her journal:

> I came out of the hospital, away from shock treatments, and strong medicine. That was about April. The three months before that are completely blank in my mind, as well as the three and a half years before April.

"They say that, after getting out of the hospital, I went through a time at home of not eating, not talking, and wanting to stay in bed all the time. Then I was referred to Dr. Rosenberg for counseling. I don't remember much of those next two or three months other than being in Dr. Rosenberg's office and talking with him.

"I'd begun 'waking up' since that first session with him. I'd begun sharing with him things that bothered me—things that I would never have dreamed of telling anyone about. And I remember how much that meant to me. It was so hard to talk. But Dr. Rosenberg cared about me and showed it, and I wanted to talk with him. I was always glad afterwards that I had let something out. I remember counting the days, even the hours, until my next appointment with him.

I've also learned that facing reality is not all bad. I am realizing more and more of the things that I need to stand up to, things that I need to get out and do on my own.

"This is scary. And it's very hard. And it's so discouraging that when I am trying really a lot, I can still fail so terribly. But the good part of reality is that I've been seeing that it includes wonderful things, too.

I've learned in the past year about how wonderful it can be to share myself with other people. I think it was mostly just one part that I learned, about the thrill of my talking to other people and have them actually listen—even really understand at times.

I continue to be amazed by the healing power of empathy. Time and again I have witnessed people transcending the paralyzing effects of psychological pain when they have sufficient contact with someone who can hear them empathically. As listeners, we don't need insights into psychological dynamics or training in

psychotherapy. What is essential is our
ability to be present to what's really going
on within—to the unique feelings and
needs a person is experiencing in that
very moment.

> **Empathy lies in our
> ability to be present.**

Summary

Our ability to offer empathy can allow us to stay vulnerable,
defuse potential violence, help us hear the word "no" without taking it as a rejection, revive a lifeless conversation, and even hear
the feelings and needs expressed through silence. Time and again
people transcend the paralyzing effects of psychological pain
when they have sufficient contact with someone who can hear
them empathically.

CHAPTER 9

Connecting Compassionately With Ourselves

Let us become the change we seek in the world.
—Mahatma Gandhi

We have seen how NVC contributes to relationships with friends and family, at work and in the political arena. Its most crucial application, however, may be in the way we treat ourselves. When we are internally violent towards ourselves, it is difficult to be genuinely compassionate towards others.

> **The most important use of NVC may be in developing self-compassion.**

Remembering The Specialness Of What We Are

In the play, "A Thousand Clowns" by Herb Gardner, the protagonist refuses to release his 12-year-old nephew to child-welfare authorities, declaring, "I want him to get to know exactly the special thing he is or else he won't notice it when it starts to go. I want him to stay awake and . . . see . . . all the wild possibilities. I want him to know it's worth all the trouble just to give the world a little goosing when you get the chance. And I want him to know the subtle, sneaky, important reason why he was born a human being and not a chair."

I am gravely concerned that many of us have lost awareness of "the special thing" we are; we have forgotten the "subtle, sneaky, important reason" the uncle so passionately wanted his nephew to know. When critical self-concepts prevent us from seeing the beauty in ourselves, we lose connection with the divine energy that is our source. Conditioned to view ourselves as objects—objects full of shortcomings—is it any wonder that many of us end up relating violently to ourselves?

An important area where this violence can be replaced with compassion is in our moment- to-moment evaluation of ourselves. Since we want whatever we do to lead to the enrichment of life, it

> **We use NVC to evaluate ourselves in ways that engender growth rather than self-hatred.**

is critical to know how to evaluate events and conditions in ways that help us learn and make ongoing choices that serve us. Unfortunately, the way we've been trained to evaluate ourselves often promotes more self-hatred than learning.

Evaluating Ourselves When We've Been Less Than Perfect

In a routine workshop activity, I ask participants to recall a recent occasion when they did something they wish they hadn't. We then look at how they spoke to themselves immediately after having made what is referred in common language as a "mistake" or "error." Typical statements were: "That was dumb!" "How could you do such an stupid thing?" "What's wrong with you?" "You're always messing up!" "That's selfish!"

These speakers have been taught to judge themselves in ways that imply that what they did was wrong or bad; their self-admonishment implicitly assumes that they deserve to suffer for what they'd done. It is tragic that so many of us get enmeshed in self-hatred rather than benefit from mistakes which show us our limitations and guide us towards growth.

Even when we sometimes do "learn a lesson" from mistakes for which we judge ourselves harshly, I worry about the nature of the energy behind that kind of change and learning. I'd like change to be stimulated by a clear desire to enrich life for ourselves or for others rather than by destructive energies such as shame or guilt.

If the way we evaluate ourselves leads us to feel shame, and we consequently change our behavior, we are allowing our growing and learning to be guided by self-hatred. Shame is a form of self-hatred, and actions taken in reaction to shame are not free and joyful acts. Even if our intention is to behave with more kindness and sensitivity, if people sense shame or guilt behind our actions, they are less likely to appreciate what we do than if we are motivated purely by the human desire to contribute to life.

In our language there is a word with enormous power to create shame and guilt. This violent word, which we commonly use to evaluate ourselves, is so deeply ingrained in our consciousness that many of us would have trouble imagining how to live without it. It is the word "should," as in "I should have known better" or "I shouldn't have done that." Most of the time when we use this word with ourselves, we resist learning because "should" implies that there is no choice. Human beings, when hearing any kind of demand, tend to resist because it

Avoid "shoulding" yourself!

threatens our autonomy—our strong need for choice. We have this reaction to tyranny even when it's internal tyranny in the form of a "should."

A similar expression of internal demand occurs in the following self-evaluation: "What I'm doing is just terrible. I really must do something about it!" Think for a moment of all the people you've heard say, "I really should give up smoking." or "I really have to do something about exercising more." They keep saying what they "must" do and they keep resisting doing it because human beings were not meant to be slaves. We were not meant to succumb to the dictates of "should" and "have to," whether they come from outside or inside of ourselves. And if we do yield and submit to these demands, our actions arise from an energy that is devoid of life-giving joy.

Translating Self-Judgments
And Inner Demands

When we communicate with ourselves on a regular basis through inner judgment, blame and demand, it's not surprising that our self-concept gives in to feeling "more like a chair than a human being." A basic premise of NVC is that whenever we imply that someone is wrong or bad, what we are really saying is that he or she is not acting in harmony with our needs. If the person we are judging happens to be ourselves, what we are saying is, "I myself am not behaving in harmony with my own needs." I am convinced that if we learn to evaluate ourselves in terms of whether and how well our needs are being fulfilled, we are much more likely to learn from the evaluation.

> Self-judgments, like all judgments, are tragic expressions of unmet needs.

Our challenge then, when we are doing something that is not enriching life, is to evaluate ourselves moment by moment in a way that inspires change both:

(1) in the direction of where we would like go, and

(2) out of respect and compassion for ourselves, rather than out of self-hatred, guilt or shame.

NVC Mourning

After a lifetime of schooling and socialization, it is probably too late for most of us to train our minds to think purely in terms of what we need and value from moment to moment. However, just as we have learned to translate judgments when conversing with others, we can train ourselves to recognize judgmental self-talk and to immediately focus our attention on the underlying needs.

For example, if we find ourselves reacting reproachfully to something we did: "Look, you just messed up again!", we can quickly stop and ask ourselves, "What unmet need of mine is being expressed through this moralistic judgment?" When we do connect to the need—and there may be several layers of needs—we will notice a remarkable shift in our bodies. Instead of the shame, guilt, or depression we likely feel when criticizing ourselves for having "messed up again," we will experience any number of feelings. Whether it's sadness, frustration, disappointment, fear, grief, or some other feeling, we have been endowed by nature with these feelings for a purpose: they mobilize us for action in pursuing and fulfilling what we need or value. Their impact on our spirit and bodies is substantially different from the disconnection that is brought on by guilt, shame, and depression.

Mourning in NVC is the process of fully connecting with the unmet needs and feelings that are generated when we have been less than perfect. It is an experience of regret, but regret that helps us learn from what we have done without blaming or hating ourselves. We see how our behavior ran counter to our own needs and values, and we open ourselves to feelings that arise out of that awareness. When our consciousness is focused on what we need, we are naturally stimulated towards the creative possibilities of how to get that need met. In contrast, the moralistic judgments we use when blaming ourselves tend to obscure such possibilities and to perpetuate a state of self-punishment.

> NVC mourning: connecting with the feelings and unmet needs stimulated by past actions which we now regret.

Self-Forgiveness

We follow up on the process of mourning with self-forgiveness. Turning our attention to the part of the self which chose to act in the way that led to the present situation, we ask ourselves, "When I behaved in the way which I now regret, what need of mine was I trying to meet?" I believe that human beings are always acting in the service of needs and values. This is true whether the action does or does not meet the need, or whether it's one we end up celebrating or regretting.

When we listen empathically to ourselves, we will be able to hear the underlying need. Self-forgiveness occurs the moment this empathic connection is made. Then we are able to recognize how

NVC self-forgiveness : connecting with the need we were trying to meet when we took the action which we now regret.

our choice was an attempt to serve life, even as the mourning process teaches us how it fell short of fulfilling our needs.

An important aspect of self-compassion is to be able to empathically hold both parts of ourselves—the self that regrets a past action and the self that took the action in the first place. The process of mourning and self-forgiveness free us in the direction of learning and growing. In connecting moment by moment to our needs, we increase our creative capacity to act in harmony with them.

The Lesson Of The Polka-Dotted Suit

I would like to illustrate the process of mourning and self-forgiveness by recalling a personal event. The day before an important workshop, I had bought a light gray summer suit to wear. At the end of the well-attended workshop, I was swarmed by participants asking for my address, signature, and other information. With time closing in on another appointment, I hastened to attend to the requests of the participants, signing and scribbling on the many bits of paper thrust in front of me. As I rushed out the door, I stuck my pen—uncapped—in the pocket of my new suit. Once outside, I discovered to my horror that instead of the nice light gray suit, I now had a polka-dotted suit!

For twenty minutes I was brutal with myself: "How could you be so careless? What a stupid thing to do!" I had just ruined a brand new suit: if ever I needed compassion and understanding, this was the time, yet here I was responding to myself in a way that left me feeling worse than ever.

Fortunately—after only twenty minutes—I noticed what I was doing. I stopped, looked for the need of mine that was unmet by having left the pen uncapped and asked myself, "What need lies behind my judging myself as 'careless' and 'stupid'"?

Immediately I saw that it was to take better care of myself: to have given more attention to my own needs while I was rushing to address everyone else's needs. As soon as I touched that part of myself and connected to the deep longing to be more aware and caring of my own needs, my feelings shifted. There was a release of tension in my body as the anger, shame and guilt I was harboring towards myself dissipated. I fully mourned the ruined suit and uncapped pen as I opened to feelings of sadness now arising along with the yearning to take better care of myself.

Next I shifted my attention to the need I was meeting when I slipped the uncapped pen in my pocket. I recognized how much I valued care and consideration for other people's needs. Of course, in taking such good care of other people's needs, I had not taken the time to do the same for myself. But instead of blame, I felt a wave of compassion for myself as I realized that even my rushing and putting the pen away unthinkingly had come out of serving my own need to respond to others in a caring way!

In that compassionate place, I am able to hold both needs: in one hand, to respond in a caring way to others' needs, and in the other, to be aware of and take better care of my own. Being conscious of both needs, I can imagine ways of behaving differently in similar situations and arriving at solutions more resourcefully than if I lose that consciousness in a sea of self-judgment.

> We are compassionate with ourselves when we are able to embrace all parts of ourselves and recognize the needs and values expressed by each part.

"Don't do anything that isn't play!"

In addition to the process of mourning and self-forgiveness, another aspect of self-compassion I emphasize is the energy behind whatever action we take. When I advise, "Don't do anything that isn't play!" some take me to be radical, even insane. I earnestly believe, however, that an important form of self-compassion is to make choices motivated purely by our desire to contribute to life rather than out of fear, guilt, shame, duty, or obligation. When we are conscious of the life-enriching purpose behind an action we

> We want to take action out of the desire to contribute to life rather than out of fear, guilt, shame, or obligation.

take, when the soul energy that motivates us is simply to make life wonderful for others and ourselves, then even hard work has an element of play in it. Correspondingly, an otherwise joyful activity performed out of obligation, duty, fear, guilt or shame will lose its joy and eventually engender resistance.

In Chapter 2, we considered replacing language that implies lack of choice with language that acknowledges choice. Many years ago I engaged in an activity which significantly enlarged the pool of joy and happiness available to my life, while diminishing depression, guilt, and shame. I offer it here as a possible way to deepen our compassion for ourselves, to help us live our lives out of joyous play by staying grounded in a clear awareness of the life-enriching need behind everything we do.

Translating "Have to" To "Choose to"

Step One

What do you do in your life that you don't experience as playful? List on a piece of paper all those things that you tell yourself you have to do, any activity you dread but do anyway because you perceive yourself to have no choice.

When I first reviewed my own list, just seeing how long it was gave me insight as to why so much of my time was spent not enjoying life. I noticed how many things in an ordinary day I was doing by tricking myself into believing that I had to do them.

The first item on my list was "write clinical reports." I hated doing these reports, yet I was spending at least an hour of agony over them every day. My second item was "drive the children's carpool to school."

Step two

After completing the list, clearly acknowledge to yourself that you are doing these things because you choose to do them, not because you have to. Insert the words "I choose to . . . " in front of each item you listed.

I recall my own resistance to this step. "Writing clinical reports," I insisted to myself, "is not something I choose to do! I have to do it. I'm a clinical psychologist. I have to write these reports."

Step three

After having acknowledged that you chose to do a particular activity, get in touch with the intention behind the choice by completing the statement, "I choose to ____ because I want ____."

At first I fumbled to identify what I wanted from writing clinical reports. Several months earlier, I had already determined that the reports did not serve my clients enough to justify the time they were taking, so why was I continuing to invest so much energy in their preparation? Finally I realized that I was choosing to write the reports solely because I wanted the income they provided. As soon as I recognized this, I never wrote another clinical report. I can't tell you how joyful I feel just thinking of how many clinical reports I haven't written since that moment 35 years ago! When I realized that money was my primary motivation, I immediately saw that I could find other ways to take care of myself financially, and that in fact, I'd rather scavenge in garbage cans for food than to write another clinical report.

The next item on my list of unjoyful tasks was driving the children to school. When I examined the reason behind that chore, however, I felt appreciation for the benefits my children received from

> With every choice you make, be conscious of what need it serves.

attending their current school. They could easily walk to the neighborhood school, but their own school was far more in harmony with my educational values. I continued to drive, but with a different energy; instead of "Oh, darn, I have to drive carpool today," I was conscious of my purpose, which was for my children to have a quality of education that was very dear to me. Of course I sometimes needed to remind myself two or three times during the drive to refocus my mind on what purpose my action was serving.

Cultivating Awareness Of The Energy Behind Our Actions

As you explore the statement, "I choose to ____ because I want ____", you may discover – as I did with the children's carpool – the important values behind the choices you've made. I am convinced that after we gain clarity regarding the need being served by our actions, we can experience them as play even when they involve hard work, challenge or frustration.

For some items on your list, however, you might uncover one or several of the following motivations:

1) FOR MONEY

Money is a major form of extrinsic reward in our society. Choices prompted by a desire for reward are costly: they deprive us of the joy in life that comes with actions grounded in the clear intention to contribute to a human need. Money is not a "need" as we define it in NVC; it is one of countless strategies that may be selected to address a need.

2) FOR APPROVAL

Like money, approval from others is a form of extrinsic reward. Our culture has educated us to hunger for reward. We attended schools that used extrinsic means to motivate us to study; we grew up in homes where we were rewarded for being good little boys and girls, and punished when our caretakers judged us to be otherwise. Thus, as adults we easily trick ourselves into believing that life consists of doing things for reward; we are addicted to getting a smile, a pat on the back, and people's verbal judgments that we are a "good person," "good parent," "good citizen," "good worker," "good friend," etc. We do things to get people to like us, and avoid things that may lead them to dislike or punish us.

I find it tragic that we work so hard to buy love and assume that we must deny ourselves and do for others in order to be liked. In fact, when we do things solely in the spirit of enhancing life, we will find others appreciating us. Their appreciation, however, is only a feedback mechanism confirming that our efforts had the intended effect. The recognition that we have chosen to use our power to serve life and have done so successfully brings us the genuine joy of celebrating ourselves in a way that approval from others can never offer.

3) TO ESCAPE PUNISHMENT

Some of us pay income tax primarily to avoid punishment. As a consequence we are likely to approach that yearly ritual with a degree of resentment. I recall, however, in my childhood how differently my father and grandfather felt about paying taxes. They had immigrated from Russia to the United States, and were desirous of supporting a government they believed were protecting people in a way that the czar had not. Imagining the many people whose welfare was being served by their tax money, they felt earnest pleasure as they sent their checks to the U.S. government.

4) TO AVOID SHAME

There may be some tasks we choose to do just to avoid shame. We know that if we don't do them, we'll end up suffering severe self-judgment, hearing our own voice telling us how there is something wrong or stupid about us. If we do something stimulated solely by the urge to avoid shame, we will generally end up detesting it.

> Be conscious of actions motivated by the desire for money or the approval of others, and by fear, shame, or guilt. Know the price you pay for them.

5) TO AVOID GUILT

In other instances, we may think, "If I don't do this, people will be disappointed in me. " We are afraid we'll end up feeling guilty for failing to fulfill other people's expectations of us. There is a world of difference between doing something for others in order to avoid guilt and doing it out of a clear awareness of our own need to contribute to the happiness of other human beings. The first is a world filled with misery; the second is a world filled with play.

6) OUT OF DUTY

When we use language which denies choice, e.g. words such as "should," "have to," "ought," "must," "can't," "supposed to," etc., our behaviors arise out of a vague sense of guilt, duty, or obligation. I consider this to be the most socially dangerous and personally unfortunate of all the ways we act when we're cut off from our needs.

In Chapter 2 we saw how the concept of "Amtssprache" allowed Adolf Eichmann and his colleagues to send tens of thousands of people to their deaths without feeling emotionally affected or personally responsible. When we speak a language that denies choice, we forfeit the life in ourselves for a robot-like mentality that disconnects us from our own core.

> The most dangerous of all behaviors may consist of doing things "because we're supposed to."

After examining the list of items you have generated, you may decide to stop doing certain things in the same spirit that I chose to forego clinical reports. As radical as it may seem, it is possible to do things only out of play. I believe that to the degree that we engage moment by moment in the playfulness of enriching life—motivated solely by the desire for its enrichment—to that degree are we being compassionate with ourselves.

Summary

The most crucial application of NVC may be in the way we treat ourselves. When we make mistakes, we can use the process of NVC mourning and self-forgiveness to show us where we can grow instead of getting caught up in moralistic self-judgments. By assessing our behaviors in terms of our own unmet needs, the impetus for change comes not out of shame, guilt, anger or depression, but out of the genuine desire to contribute to our own and others' well-being.

We also cultivate self-compassion by consciously choosing in daily life to act only in service to our own needs and values rather than out of duty, for extrinsic rewards, or to avoid guilt, shame, and punishment. If we review the joyless acts to which we currently subject ourselves and make the translation from "have to" to "choose to," we will discover more play and integrity in our lives.

CHAPTER TEN

Expressing Anger Fully

The subject of anger gives us a unique opportunity to dive more deeply into NVC. Because it brings many aspects of this process into sharp focus, the expression of anger clearly demonstrates the difference between NVC and other forms of communication.

I would like to suggest that killing people is too superficial. Killing, hitting, blaming, hurting others—whether physically or mentally—are all superficial expressions of what is going on within us when we are angry. If we are truly angry, we would want a much more powerful way to fully express ourselves.

This understanding comes as a relief to many groups I work with that experience oppression and discrimination and want to increase their power to effect change. Such groups are uneasy when they hear the terms "nonviolent" or "compassionate" communication because they have so often been urged to stifle their anger, calm down, and accept the status quo. They worry about approaches that view their anger as an undesirable quality needing to be purged. The process we are describing, however, does not encourage us to ignore, squash, or swallow anger, but rather to express the core of our anger fully and wholeheartedly.

Killing people is too superficial.

Distinguishing Stimulus From Cause

The first step to fully expressing anger in NVC is to divorce the other person from any responsibility for our anger. We rid ourselves of thoughts such as, "He, she, or they made me angry when they did

We are never angry because of what others say or do.

that." Such thinking leads us to express our anger superficially by blaming or punishing the other person. Earlier we saw that the behavior of others may be a stimulus for our feelings, but not the cause. We are never angry because of what someone else did. We can identify the other person's behavior as the stimulus, but it is important to establish a clear separation between stimulus and cause.

I'd like to illustrate this distinction with an example from my work at a Swedish prison. My job was to show prisoners who had behaved in violent ways how to fully express their anger rather than to kill, beat, or rape other people. During an exercise calling on them to identify the stimulus of their anger, one prisoner wrote: "Three weeks ago I made a request to the prison officials and they still haven't responded to it." His statement was a clear observation of a stimulus, describing what other people had done.

I then asked him to state the cause of his anger: "When this happened, you felt angry because *what*?"

"I just told you," he exclaimed. "I felt angry because they didn't respond to my request!" By equating stimulus and cause, he had tricked himself into thinking that it was the behavior of the prison officials that was making him angry. This is an easy habit to acquire in a culture that uses guilt as a means of controlling people. In such cultures, it becomes important to trick people into thinking that we can *make* others feel a certain way.

Where guilt is a tactic of manipulation and coercion, it is useful to confuse stimulus and cause. As mentioned earlier, children

To motivate by guilt, mix up stimulus and cause.

who hear, "It hurts Mommy and Daddy when you get poor grades" are led to believe that their behavior is the cause of their parents' pain. The same dynamic is observed among intimate partners: "It really disappoints me when you're not here for my birthday." The English language facilitates the use of this guilt-inducing tactic.

We say: "You make me angry." "You hurt me by doing that." "I feel sad because you did that." We use our language in many different ways to trick ourselves into believing that our feelings result from what others do. The first step in the process of fully expressing our anger is to realize that what other people do is never the cause of how we feel.

So what is the cause of anger? In Chapter 5, we discussed the four options we have when confronted with a message or behavior that we don't like.

> The cause of anger lies in our thinking—in thoughts of blame and judgment.

Anger is generated when we choose the second option: whenever we are angry, we are finding fault—we choose to play God by judging or blaming the other person for being wrong or deserving of punishment. I would like to suggest that this is the cause of anger. Even if we are not initially conscious of it, the cause of anger is located in our own thinking.

The third option described in Chapter 5 is to shine the light of consciousness on our own feelings and needs. Rather than going up to our head to make a mental analysis of wrongness regarding somebody, we choose to connect to the life that is within us. This life energy is most palpable and accessible when we focus on what we need in each moment.

For example, if someone arrives late for an appointment and we need reassurance that she cares about us, we may feel hurt. If, instead, our need is to spend time purposefully and constructively, we may feel frustrated. If, on the other hand, our need is for thirty minutes of quiet solitude, we may be grateful for her tardiness and feel pleased. Thus, it is not the behavior of the other person, but our own need that causes our feeling. When we are connected to our need, whether it is for reassurance, purposefulness, or solitude, we are in touch with our life energy. We may have strong feelings, but we are never angry. Anger is a result of life-alienating thinking that is disconnected from needs. It indicates that we have moved up to our head to analyze and judge somebody, rather than focus on which of our needs are not getting met.

In addition to the third option of focusing on our own needs and feelings, the choice is ours at any moment to shine the light of consciousness on the other person's feelings and needs. When we choose this fourth option, we also never feel anger. We are not repressing the anger; we see how anger is simply absent in each moment that we are fully present with the other person's feelings and needs.

All Anger Has A Life-Serving Core

"But," I am asked, "aren't there circumstances in which anger is justified? Isn't 'righteous indignation' called for in the face of careless, thoughtless pollution of the environment, for example?" My answer is that I strongly believe that to whatever degree I support the consciousness that there *is* such a thing as a "careless action," or a "conscientious action," a "greedy person," or a "moral person," I am contributing to violence on this planet. Rather than agreeing or disagreeing about what people *are* for murdering, raping, or polluting the environment, I believe we serve life better by focusing attention on what we are needing.

> When we judge others, we contribute to violence.

I see all anger as a result of life-alienating, violence-provocative thinking. At the core of all anger is a need that is not being fulfilled. Thus anger can be valuable if we use it as an alarm clock to wake us up—to realize we have a need that isn't being met and that we are thinking in a way that makes it unlikely to be met. To fully express anger requires full consciousness of our need. In addition, energy is required to get the need met. Anger, however, co-opts our energy by directing it toward punishing people rather than meeting our needs. Instead of engaging in "righteous indignation," I recommend connecting empathically with our own needs or those of others. This may take extensive practice, whereby over and over again, we consciously replace the phrase "I am angry because they . . . " with "I am angry *because I am needing . . . "*

> Use anger as a wake-up call.

I once was taught a remarkable lesson while working with students in a correctional school for children in Wisconsin. On two successive days I was hit on the nose in remarkably similar ways. The first time I received a sharp blow across the nose from an elbow while interceding in a fight between two students. I was so

> **Anger co-opts our energy by diverting it toward punitive actions.**

enraged it was all I could do to keep myself from hitting back. On the streets of Detroit where I grew up, it took far less than an elbow in the nose to provoke me to rage. The second day: similar situation, same nose (and thus more physical pain), but not a bit of anger!

Reflecting deeply that evening on this experience, I recognized how I had labeled the first child in my mind as a "spoiled brat." That image was in my head before his elbow ever caught my nose, and when it did, it was no longer simply an elbow hitting my nose. It was: "That obnoxious brat has no right to do this!" I had another judgment about the second child; I saw him as a "pathetic creature." Since I had a tendency to worry about this child, even though my nose was hurting and bleeding much more severely the second day, I felt no rage at all. I could not have received a more powerful lesson to help me see that it's not what the other person does, but the images and interpretations in my own head that produce my anger.

Stimulus Versus Cause: Practical Implications

I emphasize the distinction between cause and stimulus on practical and tactical as well as on philosophical grounds. I'd like to illustrate this point by returning to my dialogue with John, the Swedish prisoner:

John: "Three weeks ago I made a request to the prison officials and they still haven't responded to my request."

MBR: "So when this happened, you felt angry because *what?*"

John: "I just told you. They didn't respond to my request!"

MBR: "Hold it. Instead of saying, 'I felt angry because *they . . .*,' stop and become conscious of what you're telling yourself that's making you so angry."

John: "I'm not telling myself anything."

MBR: "Stop, slow down, just listen to what's going on inside."

John (silently reflecting and then): "I'm telling myself that they have no respect for human beings; they are a bunch of cold, faceless bureaucrats who don't give a damn about anybody but themselves! They're a real bunch of . . . "

MBR: "Thanks, that's enough. Now you know why you're angry—it's that kind of thinking."

John: "But what's wrong with thinking that way?"

MBR: "I'm not saying there is anything wrong with thinking that way. Notice if I say there is something wrong with you for thinking that way, I'd be thinking the same way about *you*. I don't say it's *wrong* to judge people, to call them faceless bureaucrats or to label their actions inconsiderate or selfish. However, it's that kind of thinking on your part that makes you feel very angry. Focus your attention on your needs: what are your needs in this situation?"

John (after a long silence): "Marshall, I need the training I was requesting. If I don't get that training, as sure as I'm sitting here, I'm gonna end up back in this prison when I get out."

MBR: "Now that your attention is on your needs, how do you feel?"

John: "Scared."

MBR: "Now put yourself in the shoes of a prison official. If I'm an inmate, am I more likely to get my needs met if I come to you saying, 'Hey I really need that training and I'm scared of what's going to happen if I don't get it . . . . ' or if I approach while seeing you as a faceless bureaucrat? Even if I don't say those words out loud, my eyes will reveal that kind of thinking. Which way am I more likely to get my needs met?"

(John, staring at floor, remains silent).

MBR: "Hey, buddy, what's going on?

John: "Can't talk about it."

> When we become aware of our needs, anger gives way to life-serving feelings.

Three hours later John approached me and said, "Marshall, I wish you had taught me two years ago what you taught me this morning. I wouldn't have had to kill my best friend."

> Violence comes from the belief that other people cause our pain and therefore deserve punishment.

All violence is the result of people tricking themselves, as did this young prisoner, into believing that their pain derives from other people and that consequently those people deserve to be punished.

One time I saw my younger son take a fifty-cent piece from his sister's room. I said, "Brett, did you ask your sister whether you could have that?" "I didn't take it from her," he answered. Now I faced my four options. I could have called him a liar, which would, however, have worked against my getting my needs met since any judgment of another person diminishes the likelihood of our needs being met. Where I focused my attention at this moment was critical. If I were to judge him as lying, it would point me in one direction. If I were to interpret that he didn't respect me enough to tell me the truth, I would be pointed in another direction. If, however, I were either to empathize with him at that moment, or express nakedly what I was feeling and needing, I would greatly increase the possibility of getting my needs met.

> We recall four options when hearing a difficult message:
> 1. Blaming ourselves
> 2. Blaming others
> 3. Sensing our own feelings and needs
> 4. Sensing others' feelings and needs

The way I expressed my choice—which in this situation turned out helpful—was not so much through what I said, but through what I did. Instead of judging him as lying, I tried to hear his feeling: he was scared, and his need was to protect himself against being punished. By empathizing with him, I had the chance of making an emotional connection out of which we could both get our needs met. However, if I had approached him with the view that he was lying—even if I hadn't expressed it out loud—he would have been less likely to feel safe expressing truthfully what had

Judgments of others contribute to self-fulfilling prophecies.

happened. I would have then become part of the process: by the very act of judging another person as a liar, I would contribute to a self-fulfilling prophecy. Why would people want to tell the truth, knowing they will be judged and punished for doing so?

I would like to suggest that when our heads are filled with judgments and analyses that others are bad, greedy, irresponsible, lying, cheating, polluting the environment, valuing profit more than life, or behaving in other ways they shouldn't, very few of them will be interested in our needs. If we want to protect the environment and we go to a corporate executive with the attitude, "You know, you are really a killer of the planet, you have no right to abuse the land in this way," we have severely impaired our chances of getting our needs met. It is a rare human being who can maintain focus on our needs when we are expressing them through images of their wrongness. Of course, we may be successful in using such judgments to intimidate people into meeting our needs. If they feel so frightened, guilty, or ashamed that they change their behavior, we may come to believe that it is possible to "win" by telling people what's wrong with them.

With a broader perspective, however, we realize that each time our needs are met in this way, we not only lose, but we have contributed very tangibly to violence on the planet. We may have solved an immediate problem, but we will have created another one. The more people hear blame and judgment, the more defensive and aggressive they become and the less they will care about our needs in the future. So even if our present need is met, in the sense that people do what we want, we will pay for it later.

Four Steps To Expressing Anger

Let's look at what the process of fully expressing our anger actually requires in concrete form. The first step is to stop and do nothing except to breathe. We refrain from making any move to blame or punish the other person. We simply stay quiet. Then we identify the thoughts that are making us angry. For example, we overhear a statement that leads us to believe that we've been excluded from a conversation because of race. We sense anger, stop and recognize the thoughts stirring in our head: "It's unfair to act like that. She's being racist." We know that all judgments

> **Steps to expressing anger:**
> 1. Stop. Breathe.
> 2. Identify our judgmental thoughts.
> 3. Connect with our needs.
> 4. Express our feelings and unmet needs.

like these are tragic expressions of unmet needs, so we take the next step and connect to the needs behind those thoughts. If I judge someone to be racist, the need may be for inclusion, equality, respect, or connection.

To fully express ourselves, we now open our mouths and speak the anger—but the anger has been transformed into needs and need-connected feelings. To articulate these feelings, however, may require a lot of courage. For me it's easy to get angry and tell people, "That was a racist thing to do!" In fact, I may even enjoy saying such things, but to get down to the deeper feelings and needs behind such a statement may be very frightening. To fully express our anger, we may say to the person, "When you entered the room and started talking to the others and didn't say anything to me and then made the comment about white people, I felt really sick to my stomach, and got so scared; it triggered off all kinds of needs on my part to be treated equally. I'd like you to tell me how you feel when I tell you this."

Offering Empathy First

In most cases, however, another step needs to take place before we can expect the other party to connect with what is going on in us. Because it will often be difficult for others to receive our feelings and needs in such situations, we would need first to empathize with them if we want them to hear us. The more we empathize with what leads them to behave in the ways that are not meeting our needs, the more likely it is that they will be able to reciprocate afterwards.

The more we hear them, the more they'll hear us.

Over the last thirty years I've had a wealth of experience speaking NVC with people who harbor strong beliefs about specific races and ethnic groups. Early one morning I was picked up by a cab at an airport to take me into town. A message from the dispatcher came over the loud speaker for the cabbie: "Pick up Mr. Fishman at the synagogue on Main Street." The man next to me in the cab muttered, "These kikes get up early in the morning so they can screw everybody out of their money."

For twenty seconds, there was smoke coming out of my ears. In earlier years, my first reaction would have been to want to physically hurt such a person. Now I took a few deep breaths and then gave myself some empathy for the hurt, fear, and rage that were stirring inside me. I attended to my feelings. I stayed conscious that my anger wasn't coming from my fellow passenger nor the statement he had just made. His comment had triggered off a volcano inside of me, but I knew that my anger and profound fear came from a far deeper source than those words he had just uttered. I sat back and simply allowed the violent thoughts to play themselves out. I even enjoyed the image of actually grabbing his head and smashing it.

Giving myself this empathy enabled me to then focus my attention on the humanness behind his message, after which the first words out of my mouth were, "Are you feeling . . . ?" I tried to empathize with him, to hear his pain. Why? Because I wanted to see the beauty in him and for him to fully apprehend what I had experienced when he made his remark. I knew I wouldn't receive that kind of understanding if there were a storm brewing inside of him. My intention was to connect with him and to show a respectful empathy for the life energy in him that was behind the comment. My experience told me that If I were able to empathize, then he would be able to hear me in return. It would not be easy, but he would be able to.

Stay conscious of the violent thoughts that arise in our minds without judging them.

"Are you feeling frustrated?" I asked.

"It appears that you might have had some bad experiences with Jewish people."

He eyed me for a moment, "Yeah! These people are disgusting, they'll do anything for money."

"You feel distrust and the need to protect yourself when you're involved in financial affairs with them?"

"That's right!" he exclaimed, continuing to release more judgments, as I listened for the feeling and need behind each one. When we settle our attention on other people's feelings and needs, we experience our common humanity. When I hear that he's scared and wants to protect himself, I recognize how I also have a need to protect myself and I too know what it's like to be scared. When my consciousness is focused on another human being's feelings and needs, I see the universality of our experience. I had a major conflict with what went on in his head, but I've learned that I enjoy human beings more if I don't hear what they think. Especially with folks who have his kind of thoughts, I've learned to savor life much more by only hearing what's going on in their hearts and not getting caught up with the stuff in their heads.

> When we hear the other person's feelings and needs, we recognize our common humanity.

This man kept on pouring out his sadness and frustration. Before I knew it, he'd finished with Jews and moved on to Blacks. He was charged with pain around a number of subjects. After nearly ten minutes of my just listening, he stopped: he had felt understood.

Then I let him know what was going on in me:

MBR: "You know, when you first started to talk, I felt a lot of anger, a lot of frustration, sadness and discouragement, because I've had very different experiences with Jews than you've had, and I was wanting you to have much more the kind of experiences I've had. Can you tell me what you heard me say?"

Man: "Oh, I'm not saying they're all . . . "

MBR: "Excuse me, hold on, hold it. Can you tell me what you heard me say?"

> **Our need is for the other person to truly hear our pain.**

Man: "What are you talking about?"

MBR: "Let me repeat what I'm trying to say. I really want you to just hear the pain I felt when I heard your words. It's really important to me that you hear that. I was saying I felt a real sense of sadness because my experiences with Jewish people have been very different. I was just wishing that you had had some experiences that were different from the ones you were describing. Can you tell me what you heard me say?"

Man: "You're saying I have no right to talk the way I did."

MBR: "No, I would like you to hear me differently. I really don't want to blame you. I have no desire to blame you."

I intended to slow down the conversation, because in my experience, to whatever degree people hear blame, they have failed to hear our pain. If this man said, "Those were terrible things for me to say; those were racist remarks I made," he would not have heard my pain. As soon as people think that they have done something wrong, they will not be fully apprehending our pain.

> **People do not hear our pain when they believe they are at fault**

I didn't want him to hear blame, because I wanted him to know what had gone on in my heart when he uttered his remark. Blaming is easy. People are used to hearing blame; sometimes they agree with it and hate themselves—which doesn't stop them from behaving the same way—and sometimes they hate us for calling them racists or whatever—which also doesn't stop their behavior. If we sense blame entering their mind, as I did in the cab, we may need to slow down, go back and hear their pain for a while more.

Taking Our Time

Probably the most important part of learning how to live the process we have been discussing is to take our time. We may feel awkward deviating from the habitual behaviors that our conditioning has rendered automatic, but if our intention is to consciously live life in harmony with our values, then we'll want to take our time.

A friend of mine, Sam Williams, jotted down the basic components of this process on a three by five card, which he would use as a "cheat sheet" at work. When his boss would confront him, Sam would stop, refer to the card in his hand, and take time to remember how to respond. When I asked whether his colleagues were finding him a little strange, constantly staring into his hand and taking so much time to form his sentences, Sam replied, "It doesn't actually take that much more time, but even if it did, it's still worth it to me. It's important for me to know that I am responding to people the way I really want to." At home he was more overt, explaining to his wife and children why he was taking the time and trouble to consult the card. Whenever there was an argument in the family, he would pull out the card and take his time. After about a month, he felt comfortable enough to put it away. Then one evening, he and Scottie, age 4, were having a conflict over television and it wasn't going well. "Daddy," Scottie said urgently, "get the card!"

For those of you wishing to apply NVC, especially in challenging situations of anger, I would suggest the following exercise. As we have seen, our anger comes from judgments, labels, and thoughts of blame, of

> **Practice translating each judgment into an unmet need.**

what people "should" do and what they "deserve." List the judgments that float most frequently in your head by using the cue, "I don't like people who are. . . . " Collect all such negative judgments in your head and then ask yourself, "When I make that judgment of a person, what am I needing and not getting?" In this way, you train yourself to frame your thinking in terms of unmet needs rather than in terms of judgments of other people.

Practice is essential, because most of us were raised, if not on the streets of Detroit, then somewhere only slightly less violent. Judging and blaming have become second nature to us. To practice NVC, we need to proceed slowly, think carefully before we speak, and often just

> **Take your time.**

take a deep breath and not speak at all. Learning the process and applying it both take time.

Summary

Blaming and punishing others are superficial expressions of anger. If we wish to fully express anger, the first step is to divorce the other person from any responsibility for our anger. Instead we shine the light of consciousness on our own feelings and needs. By expressing our needs, we are far more likely to get them met than by our judging, blaming, or punishing others.

The four steps to expressing anger are (1) stop and breathe, (2) identify our judgmental thoughts, (3) connect with our needs, and (4) express our feelings and unmet needs. Sometimes in between steps 3 and 4 we may choose to empathize with the other person so that he or she will be better able to hear us when we express ourselves in Step 4.

We need to take our time in both learning and applying the process of NVC.

NVC in Action

Parent And Teen Dialog A Life-Threatening Issue

In this situation, 15-year-old Bill took a car without permission from Jorge, a family friend. He went on a joy ride with two friends and returned the car undamaged to the garage, where its absence had not been detected. Since then, however, Jorge's 14-year-old daughter, Eva, who had gone along for the ride, told her father what had happened. Jorge then informed Bill's father, who is now approaching his son. The father has just recently been practicing NVC.

Father: So I hear you, Eva and Dave took Jorge's car without asking.

Bill: No, we didn't!

Father: *(in a loud voice)* Don't lie to me; it'll only make it worse! *(Then remembers to first connect to his own feelings and needs in order to stay in connection with his son.)* You just sit there for a moment; I need to think. *(Going inside himself, he sees how angry and scared he is. He's angry because he's telling himself, "Bill should have known better!" and "What a liar he's become!" He's scared when he thinks of all the potential consequences of not only Bill's action, but his own misjudgment of what his son might do. "That was stupid of me to assume he knows better." "Some one could have gotten killed in this!" He catches himself, "Oops, I need to translate the labels 'stupid' and 'liar' into feelings and needs. For 'stupid,' I guess the feeling is disappointment in myself: I would have liked to think that I knew him better. And as for 'liar,' I'm feeling pretty scared because I want to be able to count on getting accurate information to deal with this situation." Silence while he mulls over how to begin talking.)*

Bill, are you worried that you'd be punished if you give me accurate information?

Bill: Yeah, you're always so mean whenever I do anything you don't like.

Father: Are you saying you'd like more understanding and fairer treatment for what you do?

Bill: Oh, sure, like I'm really gonna get fair treatment and understanding from you!

Father: *(silently to himself, "Boy, do I get angry when he says that! Can't he see how hard I'm trying? I really need a little respect for how hard this is, and I guess also a little caring for how scared I'm feeling")* Sounds to me like you're worried that no matter what you say, you won't be treated fairly?

Bill: What do you care about treating me fairly? When something happens, you just want someone to punish. Besides, what's the big deal? Even if we did take the car, no one got hurt and it's back where it was. I mean, this is no major crime wave.

Father: Are you scared there'll be harsh consequences if you admit to taking the car, and you want to trust that you'll be treated justly?

Bill: Yeah.

Father: *(allowing time for silence and the connection to go deeper)* What could I do to give you that reassurance?

Bill: Promise to never punish me again.

Father: *(Aware that punishment will not help Bill develop consciousness around potential consequences of his own behavior, but will only contribute to greater disconnection and resistance, the father expresses willingness to agree to Bill's request)* I'd be open to that agreement if you agree to stay in dialogue with me. That is, we talk until I'm satisfied you're aware of all the possible consequences of your having taken that car. However, in the future, if it happens that I'm not confident that you see the potential danger of what you're in for, I might still use force—but only in order to protect you.

Bill: Wow, great! It really feels good knowing I'm so stupid you have to use force to protect me from myself!

Father: *(Losing touch with his own needs, says silently: "Man, there are times when I could just kill the little. . . . I'm so furious when he says things like that! It really doesn't seem like he cares. . . . Damn, what am I needing here? I'm needing to know, when I'm working this hard, that at least he cares.")*

(Out loud angrily) You know, Bill, when you say

things like that, I get really pissed off. I'm trying so hard to stay with you on this, and when I hear things like that. . . . Look, I need to know if you even want to keep talking with me.

Bill: I don't care.

Father: Bill, I really want to listen to you rather than fall into my old habits of blaming and threatening you whenever something comes up that I'm upset about. But when I hear you say things like, "It feels good to know I'm so stupid" in the tone of voice you just used, I find it hard to control myself. I could use your help on this. That is, if you would rather me listen to you than blame or threaten. Or if not, then, I suppose my other option is to just handle this the way I'm used to handling things.

Bill: And what would that be?

Father: Well, by now, I'd probably be saying, "Hey, you're grounded for two years: no TV, no car, no money, no dates, no nothing!"

Bill: Well, guess I'd want you to do it the new way then.

Father: *(with humor)* I'm glad to see that your sense of self-preservation is still intact. Now I need you to tell me whether you're willing to share some honesty and vulnerability.

Bill: What do you mean by "vulnerability"?

Father: It means that you tell me what you are really feeling about the things we're talking about, and I tell you the same from my end. *(In a firm voice)* Are you willing?

Bill: Okay, I'll try.

Father: *(with sigh of relief)* Thank you. I'm grateful for your willingness to try. Did I tell you—Jorge grounded Eva for three months—she won't be allowed to do anything. How do you feel about that?

Bill: Oh man, what a bummer; that's so unfair!

Father: I'd like to hear how you really feel about it.

Bill: I told you—it's totally unfair!

Father: *(realizing Bill isn't in touch with what he's feeling, decides to guess)* Are you sad that she's having to pay so much for her mistake?

Bill: No, it's not that. I mean, it wasn't her mistake really.

Father: Oh, so are you upset she's paying for something that was your idea to start with?

Bill: Well, yeah, she just went along with what I told her to do.

Father: Sounds to me like you're kind of hurting inside seeing the kind of effect your decision had on Eva.

Bill: Sorta.

Father: Billy, I really need to know that you are able to see how your actions have consequences.

Bill: Well, I wasn't thinking about what could've gone wrong. Yeah, I guess I did really screw up bad.

Father: I'd rather you see it as something you did that didn't turn out the way you wanted. And I still need reassurance about your being aware of the consequences. Would you tell me what you're feeling right now about what you did?

Bill: I feel really stupid, Dad . . . I didn't mean to hurt anyone.

Father: *(translating Bill's self-judgments into feelings and needs)* So you're sad, and regret what you did because you'd like to be trusted not to do harm?

Bill: Yeah, I didn't mean to cause so much trouble. I just didn't think about it.

Father: Are you saying you wish you had thought about it more and gotten clearer before you acted?

Bill: *(reflecting)* Yeah . . .

Father: Well, it's reassuring for me to hear that, and for there to be some real healing with Jorge, I would like you to go to him and tell him what you just told me. Would you be willing to do that?

Bill: Oh man, that's so scary; he'll be really mad!

Father: Yeah, it's likely he will be. That's one of the consequences. Are you willing to be responsible for your actions? I like Jorge and I want to keep him for a friend, and I'm guessing that you would like to keep your connection with Eva. Is that the case?

Bill: She's one of my best friends.

Father: So shall we go see them?

Bill: *(fearfully and reluctantly)* Well. . . okay. Yeah, I guess so.

Father: Are you scared and needing to know that you will be safe if you go there?

Bill: Yeah.

Father: We'll go together: I'll be there for you and with you. I'm really proud that you are willing.

CHAPTER ELEVEN

The Protective Use Of Force

When The Use Of Force Is Unavoidable

When two disputing parties have each had an opportunity to fully express what they are observing, feeling, needing, and requesting—and each has empathized with the other—a resolution can usually be reached that meets the needs of both sides. At the very least, the two can agree, in goodwill, to disagree.

In some situations, however, the opportunity for such dialogue may not exist, and the use of force may be necessary to protect life or individual rights. For instance, the other party may be unwilling to communicate, or imminent danger may not allow time for communication. In these situations, we may need to resort to force. If we do, NVC requires us to differentiate between the protective and the punitive uses of force.

The Thinking Behind The Use Of Force

The intention behind the protective use of force is to prevent injury or injustice. The intention behind the punitive use of force is to cause individuals to suffer for their perceived misdeeds. When we grab a child who is running into the street to prevent the child from being injured, we are applying protective force. The punitive use of force, on the other hand, might involve physical or psychological attack, such as spanking the child or reproofs like, "How could you be so stupid! You should be ashamed of yourself!"

When we exercise the protective use of force, we are focusing

> The intention behind the protective use of force is only to protect, not to punish, blame, or condemn.

on the life or rights we want to protect without passing judgment on either the person or the behavior. We are not blaming or condemning the child rushing into the street; our thinking is solely directed toward protecting the child from danger. (For application of this kind of force in social and political conflicts, see Robert Irwin's book, Nonviolent Social Defense.) The assumption behind the protective use of force is that people behave in ways injurious to themselves and others due to some form of ignorance. The corrective process is therefore one of education, not punishment. Ignorance includes (a) a lack of awareness of the consequences of our actions, (b) an inability to see how our needs may be met without injury to others, (c) the belief that we have the "right" to punish or hurt others because they "deserve" it, and (d) delusional thinking that involves, for example, hearing a "voice" that instructs us to kill someone.

Punitive action, on the other hand, is based on the assumption that people commit offenses because they are bad or evil, and to correct the situation, they need to be made to repent. Their "correction" is undertaken through punitive action designed to make them (1) suffer enough to see the error of their ways, (2) repent, and (3) change. In practice, however, punitive action, rather than evoking repentance and learning, is just as likely to generate resentment and hostility and to reinforce resistance to the very behavior we are seeking.

Types Of Punitive Force

Physical punishment, such as spanking, is one punitive use of force. I have found the subject of corporal punishment to provoke strong sentiments among parents. Some adamantly defend the practice, while referring to the Bible: "Spare the rod, spoil the child. It's because parents don't spank that delinquency is now rampant." They are persuaded that spanking our children shows that we love them by setting clear boundaries. Other parents are equally insistent that spanking is unloving and ineffective because it teaches children that, when all else fails, we can always resort to physical violence.

My personal concern is that children's fear of corporal punishment may obscure their awareness of the compassion that underlies parental demands. Parents often tell me that they "have to" use punitive force because they see no other way to influence their children to do "what's good for them." They support their opinion with anecdotes of children expressing appreciation for "seeing the light" after having been punished. Having raised four children, I empathize deeply with parents regarding the daily challenges they face in educating children and keeping them safe. This does not, however, lessen my concern about the use of physical punishment.

> Fear of corporal punishment obscures children's awareness of the compassion underlying parental demands.

First, I wonder whether people who proclaim the successes of such punishment are aware of the countless instances of children who turn against what might be good for them simply because they choose to fight, rather than succumb, to coercion. Second, the apparent success of corporal punishment in influencing a child doesn't mean that other methods of influence wouldn't have worked equally well. Finally, I share the concerns of many parents about the social consequences of using physical punishment. When parents opt to use force, we may win the battle of getting children to do what we want, but in the process, are we not perpetuating a social norm that justifies violence as a means of resolving differences?

In addition to the physical, other uses of force also qualify as punishment. One is the use of blame to discredit another person: for example, a parent may label a child as "wrong," "selfish," or "immature" when a child doesn't behave in a certain way. Another form of punitive force is the withholding of some means of gratification, such as parents' curtailing of allowance or

> Punishment also includes judgmental labeling and the withholding of privileges.

driving privileges. In this type of punishment, the withdrawal of caring or respect is one of the most powerful threats of all.

The Costs Of Punishment

When we submit to doing something solely for the purpose of avoiding punishment, our attention is distracted from the value of the action itself. Instead, we are focusing upon the consequences of what might happen if we fail to take that action. If a worker's performance is prompted by fear of punishment, the job gets done, but morale suffers; sooner or later, productivity will decrease. Self-esteem is also diminished when punitive force is used. If children brush their teeth because they fear shame and ridicule, their oral health may improve but their self-respect will develop cavities. Furthermore, as we all know, punishment is costly in terms of goodwill. The more we are seen as agents of punishment, the harder it is for others to respond compassionately to our needs.

> When we fear punishment, we focus on consequences, not on our own values.
>
> Fear of punishment diminishes self-esteem and goodwill.

I was visiting a friend, a school principal, at his office when he noticed through the window a big child hitting a smaller one. "Excuse me," he said as he leapt up and rushed to the playground. Grabbing the larger child, he gave him a swat and scolded, "I'll teach you not to hit smaller people!" When the principal returned inside, I remarked, "I don't think you taught that child what you thought you were teaching him. I suspect what he learned instead was not to hit people smaller than he is when somebody bigger—like the principal—might be watching! If anything, it seems to me that you have reinforced the notion that the way to get what you want from somebody else is to hit them."

In such situations, I recommend first empathizing with the child who is behaving violently. For example, if I saw a child hit someone after being called a name, I might empathize, "I'm sensing that you're feeling angry because you'd like to be treated with more respect." If I guessed correctly, and the child acknowledges this to be true, I would then continue by expressing my own feelings, needs, and requests in this situation without insinuating blame: "I'm feeling sad because I want us to find ways to get respect that don't turn people into enemies. I'd like you to tell me if you'd be willing to explore with me some other ways to get the respect you're wanting."

Two Questions That Reveal The Limitations Of Punishment

Two questions help us see why we are unlikely to get what we want by using punishment to change people's behavior. The first question is: *What do I want this person to do that's different from what he or she is currently doing?* If we ask only this first question, punishment may seem effective because the threat or exercise of punitive force may well influence the person's behavior. However, with the second question, it becomes evident that punishment isn't likely to work: *What do I want this person's reasons to be for doing what I'm asking?*

We seldom address the latter question, but when we do, we soon realize that punishment and reward interfere with people's ability to do things motivated by the reasons we'd like them to have. I believe it is critical to be aware of the importance of people's reasons for behaving as we request. For example, blaming or punishing would obviously not be effective strategies if we want children to clean their rooms out of either a desire for order or a desire to contribute to the parents' enjoyment of order. Often children clean their rooms motivated by obedience to authority ("Because my Mom said so"), avoidance of punishment, or fear of upsetting or being rejected by parents. NVC, however, fosters a level of moral development based on autonomy and interdependence, whereby we acknowledge responsibility for our own actions and are aware

> Question 1: What do I want this person to do?
>
> Question 2: What do I want this person's reasons to be for doing it?

that our own well-being and that of others are one and the same.

The Protective Use Of Force In Schools

I'd like to describe how some students and I used protective force to bring order into a chaotic situation at an alternative school. This school was designed for students who had dropped out or been expelled from conventional classrooms. The administration and I hoped to demonstrate that a school based on the principles of NVC would be able to reach these students. My job was to train the faculty in NVC and serve as consultant over the year. With only four days to prepare the faculty, I was unable to sufficiently clarify the difference between NVC and permissiveness. As a result, some teachers were ignoring, rather than intervening, in situations of conflict and disturbing behavior. Besieged by increasing pandemonium, the administrators were nearly ready to shut down the school.

When I requested to talk with the students who had contributed most to the turbulence, the principal selected eight boys, ages eleven to fourteen, to meet with me. The following are excerpts from the dialogue I had with the students.

> MBR: *(Expressing my feeling and needs without asking probing questions.)* I'm very upset about the teachers' reports that things are getting out of hand in many of the classes. I want very much for this school to be successful. I'm hopeful that you can help me understand what the problems are and what can be done about them.
>
> Will: The teachers in this school—they fools, man!
>
> MBR: Are you saying, Will, that you are disgusted with the teachers and you want them to change some things they do?
>
> Will: No, man, they is fools because they just stand around and don't do nothin'.
>
> MBR: You mean you're disgusted because you want them to do more when problems happen. *(This is a second attempt*

to receive the feelings and wants.)

Will: That's right, man. No matter what anybody do they just stand there smilin' like fools.

MBR: Would you be willing to give me an example of how the teachers do nothing?

Will: Easy. Just this morning a dude walks in wearin' a bottle of Wild Turkey on his hip pocket plain as day. Everybody seen it; the teacher, she seen it but she's lookin' the other way.

MBR: It sounds to me, then, that you don't have respect for the teachers when they stand around doing nothing. You'd like them to do something. *(This is a continued attempt to fully understand.)*

Will: Yeah.

MBR: I feel disappointed because I want them to be able to work things out with students but it sounds like I wasn't able to show them what I meant.

The discussion then turned to one particularly pressing problem, that of students who didn't want to work disturbing those who did.

MBR: I'm anxious to try to solve this problem because the teachers tell me it's the one that bothers them the most. I would appreciate your sharing whatever ideas you have with me.

Joe: The teacher got to get a rattan *(a stick covered with leather that was carried by some principals in St. Louis to administer corporal punishment).*

MBR: So you're saying, Joe, that you want the teachers to hit students when they bother others.

Joe: That's the only way students gonna stop playing the fool.

MBR: So you doubt that any other way would work. *(Still trying to receive Joe's feelings.)*

Joe: *(Nods agreement.)*

MBR: I'm discouraged if that's the only way. I hate that way of settling things and want to learn other ways.

Ed: Why?

MBR: Several reasons. Like if I get you to stop horsing around in school by using the rattan, I'd like you to tell me what happens if three or four of you that I've hit in class are out by my car when I go home.

Ed: *(Smiling)* Then you better have a big stick, man!

MBR: *(Feeling certain I understood Ed's message and certain he knew I understood, I continue without paraphrasing it.)* That's what I mean. I'd like you to see I'm bothered about that way of settling things. I'm too absentminded to always remember to carry a big stick, and even if I remembered, I would hate to hit someone with it.

Ed: You could kick the cat out of school.

MBR: You're suggesting, Ed, that you would like us to suspend or expel kids from the school?

Ed: Yeah.

MBR: I'm discouraged with that idea, too. I want to show that there are other ways of solving differences in school without kicking people out. I'd feel like a failure if that was the best we could do.

Will: If a dude ain't doin' nothing, how come you can't put him in a do-nothin' room?

MBR: Are you suggesting, Will, that you would like to have a room to send people to if they bother other students?

Will: That's right. No use they bein' in class if they ain't doin' nothin'.

MBR: I'm very interested in that idea. I'd like to hear how you think such a room might work.

Will: Sometimes you come to school and just feel evil: you don't want to do nothin'. So we just have a room students go to till they feel like doin' somethin'.

MBR: I understand what you are saying, but I'm anticipating that the teacher will be concerned about whether the students will go willingly to the do-nothing room.

Will: *(Confidently)* They'll go.

I said I thought the plan might work if we could show that the purpose was not to punish, but to provide a place to go for those who weren't ready to study, and simultaneously a chance to study for those who wanted to study. I also suggested that a do-nothing room would be more likely to succeed if it was known to be a product of student brainstorming rather than staff decree.

A do-nothing room was set up for students who were upset and didn't feel like doing schoolwork or whose behavior kept others from learning. Sometimes students asked to go; sometimes teachers asked students to go. We placed the teacher who had best mastered NVC in the do-nothing room, where she had some very productive talks with the children who came in. This set-up was an immense success in restoring order to the school because the students who devised it made its purpose clear to their peers: to protect the rights of students who wanted to learn. We used the dialogue with the students to demonstrate to the teachers that there were other means of resolving conflicts besides withdrawal from the conflict or using punitive force.

Summary

In situations where there is no opportunity for communication, such as in instances of imminent danger, we may need to resort to the protective use of force. The intention behind the protective use of force is to prevent injury or injustice, never to punish or to cause individuals to suffer, repent, or change. The punitive use of force tends to generate hostility and to reinforce resistance to the very behavior we are seeking. Punishment damages goodwill and self-esteem, and shifts our attention from the intrinsic value of an action to external consequences. Blaming and punishing fail to contribute to the motivations we would like to inspire in others.

Humanity
has been sleeping
—and still sleeps—
lulled within the
narrowly confining
joys of its
closed loves.

—Teilhard de Chardin
Theologian

CHAPTER TWELVE

Liberating Ourselves and Counseling Others

Freeing Ourselves From Old Programming

We've all learned things that limit us as human beings, whether from well-intentioned parents, teachers, clergy, or others. Passed down through generations, even centuries, much of this destructive cultural learning is so ingrained in our lives that we are no longer conscious of it. In one of his routines, comedian Buddy Hackett, raised on his mother's rich cooking, claimed that he never realized it was possible to leave the table without feeling heartburn until he was in the army. In the same way, pain engendered by damaging cultural conditioning is such an integral part of our lives that we can no longer distinguish its presence. It takes tremendous energy and awareness to recognize this destructive learning and to transform it into thoughts and behaviors that are of value and of service to life.

This requires a literacy of needs and the ability to get in touch with ourselves, both of which are difficult for people in our culture. Not only have we never been educated to be literate about our needs, we are often exposed to cultural training that actively blocks our consciousness in this way. As mentioned earlier, we have inherited a language that served kings and powerful elites in domination societies. The masses, discouraged from developing awareness of their own needs, have instead been educated to be docile and subservient to authority. Our culture implies that needs are negative and destructive; the word "needy" applied to a person suggests inadequacy or immaturity. When people express their needs, they are often labeled "selfish" and the use of the personal pronoun "I" is at times equated with selfishness or neediness.

By encouraging us to separate observation and evaluation, to acknowledge the thoughts or needs shaping our feelings, and to express our requests in clear action language, NVC heightens our awareness of the cultural conditioning influencing us at any given moment. And drawing this conditioning into the light of consciousness is a key step in breaking its hold on us.

> We can liberate ourselves from cultural conditioning.

Resolving Internal Conflicts

We can apply NVC to resolve the internal conflicts that often result in depression. In his book, *Revolution in Psychiatry*, Ernest Becker attributes depression to "cognitively arrested alternatives." This means that when we have a judgmental dialogue going on within, we become alienated from what we are needing and cannot then act to meet those needs. Depression is indicative of a state of alienation from our own needs.

A woman studying NVC was suffering a profound bout of depression. She was asked to identify the voices within her when she felt the most depressed and to write them down in dialogue form as though they were speaking to each other. The first two lines of her dialogue were:

Voice 1 ("career woman"): I should do something more with my life. I'm wasting my education and talents.

Voice 2 ("responsible mother"): You're being unrealistic. You're a mother of two children and can't handle *that* responsibility, so how can you handle anything else?"

Notice how these inner messages are infested with judgmental terms and phrases such as "should," "wasting my education and talents," and "can't handle." Variations of this dialogue had been running for months in the woman's head. She was then asked to imagine the "career woman" voice taking an "NVC pill" in order to restate its message in the following form: "When _a_, I feel _b_, because I am needing _c_. Therefore I now would like _d_."

She subsequently translated "I should do something with my life. I'm wasting my education and talents" into: "*When* I spend as much time at home with the children as I do without practicing my profession, *I feel* depressed and discouraged *because I am needing* the fulfillment I once had in my profession. *Therefore, I now would like* to find part-time work in my profession."

Then it was the turn of her "responsible mother" voice to undergo the same process. The lines, "You're being unrealistic. You're a mother of two children and can't handle *that* responsibility, so how can you handle anything else?" were transformed into: "*When* I imagine going to work, *I feel* scared *because I'm needing* reassurance that the children will be well taken care of. *Therefore, I now would like* to plan how to provide high-quality child care while I work and how to find sufficient time to be with the children when I am not tired."

This woman felt great relief as soon as she translated her inner messages into NVC. She was able to get beneath the alienating messages she was repeating to herself and offer herself empathy. Although she still faced practical challenges such as securing quality child care and her husband's support, she was no longer subject to the judgmental internal dialogue that kept her from being aware of her own needs.

> To be able to hear our own feelings and needs and to empathize with them can free us from depression.

Caring For Our Inner Environment

When we are entangled in critical, blaming, or angry thoughts, it is difficult to establish a healthy internal environment for ourselves. NVC helps us create a more peaceful state of mind by encouraging us to focus on what we are truly wanting rather than on what is wrong with others or ourselves.

A participant once reported a profound personal breakthrough during a three-day training. One of her goals for the workshop was to take better care of herself, but she woke at dawn the second morning with the worst headache in recent memory. "Normally, the first thing I'd do would be to analyze what I had done wrong. Did I eat the wrong food? Did l let myself get stressed-out? Did I do this; did I not do that? But, since I had been working on using NVC to take better care of myself, I asked instead, 'What do I need to do for myself right now with this headache?'

> Focus on what we want to do rather than what went wrong.

"I sat up and did a lot of really slow neck rolls, then got up and walked around, and did other things to take care of myself right then instead of beating up on myself. My headache relaxed to the point where I was able to go through the day's workshop. This was a major, major breakthrough for me. What I understood, when I empathized with the headache, was that I hadn't given myself enough attention the day before, and the headache was a way to say to myself, 'I need more attention.' I ended up giving myself the attention I needed and was then able to make it through the workshop. I've had headaches all my life, and this was a very remarkable turning point for me."

At another workshop a participant asked how NVC might be used to free us from anger-provoking messages when we are driving on the freeway. This was a familiar topic for me! For years my work involved traveling by car across the country, and I was worn and frazzled by the violence-provoking messages racing through my brain. Everybody who wasn't driving by my standards was an archenemy, a villain. Thoughts spewed through my head: "What the hell is the matter with that guy!? Doesn't he even watch where he's driving?" In this state of mind, all I wanted was to punish the other driver, and since I couldn't do that, the anger lodged in my body and exacted its toll.

Eventually I learned to translate my judgments into feelings and needs and to give myself empathy, "Boy, I am petrified when people drive like that; I really wish they would see the danger in what they are doing!" Whew! I was amazed how less stressful a situation I could create for myself by simply becoming aware of what I was feeling and needing rather than blaming others.

> Defuse stress by hearing our own feelings and needs.

Later I decided to practice empathy toward other drivers and was rewarded with a gratifying first experience. I was stuck behind a car going far below the speed limit that was slowing down at every intersection. Fuming and grumbling, "That's no way to drive," I noticed the stress I was causing myself and shifted my thinking instead to what the driver might be feeling and needing. I sensed that the person was lost, feeling confused, and wishing for some patience from those of us following. When the road widened enough for me to pass, I saw that the driver was a woman who looked to be in her

> Defuse stress by empathizing with others.

80's who wore an expression of terror on her face. I was pleased that my attempt at empathy had kept me from honking the horn or engaging in my customary tactics of displaying displeasure toward people whose driving bothered me.

Replacing Diagnosis With NVC

Many years ago, after having just invested nine years of my life in the training and diplomas necessary to qualify as a psychotherapist, I came across a dialogue between the Israeli philosopher Martin Buber and the American psychologist Carl Rogers, in which Buber questions whether anyone could do psychotherapy in the role of a psychotherapist. Buber was visiting the United States at the time, and had been invited, along with Carl Rogers, to a discussion at a mental hospital in front of a group of mental-health professionals.

In this dialogue Buber posits that human growth occurs through a meeting between two individuals who express themselves vulnerably and authentically in what he termed an "I-Thou" relationship. He did not believe that this type of authenticity was likely to exist when people meet in the roles of psychotherapist and client. Rogers agreed that authenticity was a prerequisite to growth. He maintained, however, that enlightened psychotherapists could choose to transcend their own role and encounter their clients authentically.

Buber was skeptical. He was of the opinion that even if psychotherapists were committed and able to relate to their clients in an authentic fashion, such encounters would be impossible as long as clients continued to view themselves as clients and their psychotherapists as psychotherapists. He observed how the very process of making appointments to see someone at their office, and paying fees to be "fixed," dimmed the likelihood of an authentic relationship developing between two persons.

This dialogue clarified my own longstanding ambivalence toward clinical detachment—a sacrosanct rule in the psychoanalytic psychotherapy I was taught. To bring one's own feelings and needs into the psychotherapy was typically viewed as a sign of pathology on the part of the therapist. Competent psychotherapists were to stay out of the therapy process and to function as a mirror onto which clients projected their transferences, which were then worked through with the psychotherapist's help. I understood the theory behind keeping the psychotherapist's inner process out of psychotherapy and guarding against the danger of addressing internal conflicts at the client's expense. However, I had always been uncomfortable maintaining the requisite emotional distance, and furthermore believed in the advantages of bringing myself into the process.

I thus began to experiment by replacing clinical language with the language of NVC. Instead of interpreting what my clients were saying in line with personality theories I had studied, I made myself present to their words and listened empathically. Instead of diagnosing them, I revealed what was going on within myself. At first, this was frightening. I worried about how colleagues would react to the authenticity with which I was entering into dialogue with clients. However, the results were so gratifying to both the clients and myself that I soon overcame any hesitation. Since 1963, the concept of bringing oneself fully into the client-therapist relationship has

> I empathized with clients instead of interpreting them; I revealed myself instead of diagnosing them.

ceased being heretical, but when I began practicing this way I was often invited to speak by groups of psychotherapists who would challenge me to demonstrate this new role.

Once I was asked by a large gathering of mental health professionals at a state mental hospital to show how NVC might serve in counseling distressed people. After my one-hour presentation, I was requested to interview a patient in order to produce an evaluation and recommendation for treatment. I talked with the 29-year-old mother of three children for about half an hour. After she left the room, the staff responsible for her care posed their questions. "Dr. Rosenberg," her psychiatrist began, "please make a differential diagnosis. In your opinion, is this woman manifesting a schizophrenic reaction or is this a case of drug-induced psychosis?"

I said that I was uncomfortable with such questions. Even when I worked in a mental hospital during my training, I was never sure how to fit people into the diagnostic classifications. Since then I had read research indicating a lack of agreement among psychiatrists and psychologists regarding these terms. The reports concluded that diagnoses of patients in mental hospitals depended more upon the school the psychiatrist had attended than the characteristics of the patients themselves.

I would be reluctant, I continued, to apply these terms even if consistent usage did exist, because I failed to see how they benefited patients. In physical medicine, pinpointing the disease process that has created the illness often gives clear direction to its treatment, but I did not perceive this relationship in the field we call mental illness. In my experience, during case conferences at hospitals, the staff would spend most of its time deliberating over a diagnosis. As the allotted hour threatened to run out, the psychiatrist in charge of the case might appeal to the others for help in setting up a treatment plan. Often this request would be ignored in favor of continued wrangling over the diagnosis.

I explained to the psychiatrist that NVC urges me to ask myself the following questions rather than think in terms of what is wrong with a patient: "What is this person feeling? What is she or he needing? How am I feeling in response to this person, and what needs of mine are behind my feelings? What action or decision would I request this person to take in the belief that it would enable them to live more happily?" Because our responses to these questions would reveal a lot about ourselves and our values, we would feel far more vulnerable than if we were to simply diagnose the other person.

On another occasion, I was called to demonstrate how NVC could be taught to people diagnosed as chronic schizophrenics. With about 80 psychologists, psychiatrists, social workers, and nurses watching, 15 patients who had been thus diagnosed were assembled on the stage for me. As I introduced myself and explained the purpose of NVC, one of the patients expressed a reaction that seemed irrelevant to what I was saying. Aware that he'd been diagnosed as a chronic schizophrenic, I succumbed to clinical thinking by assuming that my failure to understand him was due to his confusion. "You seem to have trouble following what I'm saying," I remarked.

At this, another patient interjected, "I understand what he's saying," and proceeded to explain the relevance of his words in the context of my introduction. Recognizing that the man was not confused, but that I had simply not grasped the connection between our thoughts, I was dismayed by the ease with which I had attributed responsibility for the breakdown in communication to him. I would have liked to have owned my own feelings by saying, for example, "I'm confused. I'd like to see the connection between what I said and your response, but I don't. Would you be willing to explain how your words relate to what I said?"

With the exception of this brief departure into clinical thinking, the session with the patients went successfully. The staff, impressed with the patients' responses, wondered whether I considered them to be an unusually cooperative group of patients. I answered that when I avoided diagnosing people and instead stayed connected to the life going on in them and in myself, people usually responded positively.

A staff member then requested a similar session to be conducted as a learning experience with some of the psychologists and psychiatrists as participants. At this, the patients who had been on stage exchanged seats with several volunteers in the audience. In working with the staff, I had a difficult time clarifying to one psychiatrist the difference between intellectual understanding and the empathy of NVC. Whenever someone in the group expressed feelings, he would offer his understanding of the psychological dynamics behind their feelings rather than empathize with the feelings. When this happened for the third time, one of the patients in the audience burst out, "Can't you see you're doing it again? You're interpreting what she's saying rather than empathizing with her feelings!"

By adopting the skills and consciousness of NVC, we can counsel others in encounters that are genuine, open, and mutual, rather than resorting to professional relationships characterized by emotional distancing, diagnosis, and hierarchy.

Summary

NVC enhances inner communication by helping us translate negative internal messages into feelings and needs. Our ability to distinguish our own feelings and needs and to empathize with them can free us from depression. We can then recognize the existence of choice in all our actions. By showing us how to focus on what we truly want rather than on what is wrong with others or ourselves, NVC gives us the tools and understanding to create a more peaceful state of mind. Professionals in counseling and psychotherapy may also use NVC to engender relationships with clients that are mutual and authentic.

NVC in Action

Dealing With Resentments And Self-Judgment

A student of Nonviolent Communication shares the following story.

I had just returned from my first residential training in NVC. A friend whom I hadn't seen for two years was waiting for me at home. I first met Iris, who has been a school librarian for 25 years, during an intense 2-week heartwork and wilderness journey that had culminated in a 3-day solo fast in the Rockies. After she listened to my enthusiastic description of NVC, Iris revealed that she was still hurting from what one of the wilderness leaders in Colorado had said to her six years ago. I had a clear memory of that person: wild woman Leav, her palms gouged with rope cuts holding steady a belayed body dangling against the mountain face; she read animal droppings, howled in the dark, danced her joy, cried her truth and mooned our bus as we waved goodbye for the last time. What Iris had heard Leav say during one of the personal feedback sessions was this: "Iris, I can't stand people like you, always and everywhere being so damn nice and sweet, constantly the meek little librarian that you are. Why don't you just drop it and get on with it?"

For six years Iris had been listening to Leav's voice in her head and for six years she'd been answering Leav in her head. We were both eager to explore how a consciousness of NVC would have affected this situation. I role-played Leav and repeated her statement to Iris.

Iris: (*forgetting about NVC, hears criticism and put-down*) You have no right to say that to me. You don't know who I am, or what kind of librarian I am! I take my profession seriously, and for your information, I consider myself to be an educator, just like any teacher . . .

I: *(with NVC consciousness, listening empathically, as if I were Leav)* It sounds to me like you're angry because you want me to know and recognize who you really are before criticizing you. Is that so?

Iris: That's right! You have simply no idea how much it took for me to even sign up for this trek. Look! Here I am: I finished, didn't I? I took on all the challenges these fourteen days and overcame them all!

I as Leav: Am I hearing that you feel hurt and would have liked some recognition and appreciation for all your courage and hard work?

A few more exchanges follow, whereupon Iris shows a shift; these shifts can often be observed bodily when a person feels "heard" to his or her satisfaction. For instance, a person may relax and take a deeper breath at this moment. This often indicates that the person has received adequate empathy and is now able to shift attention to something other than the pain they have been expressing. Sometimes they are ready to hear another person's feelings and needs. Or sometimes another round of empathy is needed to attend to another area of pain in the person. In this situation with Iris, I could see that another piece needed attention before she would be able to hear Leav. This is because Iris had had 6 years of opportunity to put herself down for not having produced an honorable comeback on the spot. After the subtle shift, she immediately went on:

Iris: Darn, I should have said all this stuff to her six years ago!

I: *(as myself, an empathic friend)* You're frustrated because you wish you could have articulated yourself better at the time?

> *Iris:* I feel like such an idiot! I knew I wasn't a "meek lit-tle librarian," but why didn't I say that to her?
>
> *I:* So you wish you had been enough in touch with yourself to say that?
>
> *Iris:* Yes. And I'm also mad at myself! I wish I hadn't let her push me around.
>
> *I:* You'd like to have been more assertive than you were?
>
> *Iris:* Exactly, I need to remember I have a right to stand up for who I am.
>
> Iris is quiet for a few seconds. She expresses readiness to practice NVC and hear what Leav said to her in a different way.
>
> *I as Leav:* Iris, I can't stand people like you, always so nice and sweet, being forever the meek little librarian. Why don't you just drop it and get on with it?
>
> *Iris:* *(listening for Leav's feelings, needs and requests)* Oh, Leav, it sounds to me like you're really frustrated . . . frustrated because . . . because I . . . *(Here Iris catches herself at a common mistake. By using the word "I," she attributes Leav's feeling to Iris herself, rather than to some desire on Leav's own part that generates the feeling, i.e. not "You're frustrated because I am a certain way," but "You're frustrated because you wanted something different from me.")*
>
> *(She tries again)* Okay, Leav, it sounds like you're really frustrated because you are wanting . . . um . . . you're wanting. . . .
>
> As I tried in my role-play to earnestly identify with Leav, I felt a sudden flash of awareness of what I *(as Leav)* was yearning for: "Connection! . . . That's what I am wanting! I want to feel connected. . . . with you, Iris! And I am so frustrated with all the sweetness and niceness that stand

in the way that I just want to tear it all down so I can truly touch you!"

We both sat a bit stunned after this outburst, and then Iris said, "If I had known that's what she had wanted, if she could have told me that it was genuine connection with me she was after. . . . Gosh, I mean, that feels almost loving." While she never did find the real Leav to verify the insight, after this practice session in NVC, Iris achieved an internal resolution about this nagging conflict and found it easier to hear with a new awareness when people around her said things to her that she might previously have interpreted as "put-downs."

. . . the more you become a connoisseur of gratitude, the less you are a victim of resentment, depression, and despair. Gratitude will act as an elixir that will gradually dissolve the hard shell of your ego—your need to possess and control—and transform you into a generous being. The sense of gratitude produces true spiritual alchemy, makes us magnanimous— large souled.

—Sam Keen

CHAPTER THIRTEEN

Expressing Appreciation In Nonviolent Communication

The Intention Behind The Appreciation

"You did a good job on that report."

"You are a very sensitive person."

"It was kind of you to offer me a ride home last evening."

Such statements are typically uttered as expressions of appreciation in life-alienating communication. Perhaps you are surprised that I regard praise and compliments to be life-alienating. Notice, however, that appreciation expressed in this form reveals little of what's going on in the speaker and establishes the speaker as someone who sits in judgment. I define judgments—both positive and negative—as life-alienating communication.

> Compliments are often judgments—however positive—of others.

In the corporate trainings we offer, I often encounter managers who defend the practice of praising and complimenting by claiming that "it works." "Research shows," they assert, "that if a manager compliments employees, they work harder. And the same goes for schools: if teachers praise students, they study harder." Although I have reviewed this research, my belief is that recipients of such praise do work harder, but only initially. Once they sense the manipulation behind the appreciation, their productivity drops.

What is most disturbing for me, however, is that the beauty of appreciation is spoiled when people begin to notice the lurking intent to get something out of them.

Furthermore, when we use positive feedback as a means to influence others, it may not be clear how they are receiving the message. There is a cartoon where one Native American remarks to another, "Watch me use modern psychology on my horse!" He then leads his friend near to where the horse can overhear their conversation and exclaims, "I have the fastest, most courageous horse in all the West!" The horse looks sad and says to itself, "How do you like that? He's gone and bought himself another horse."

Express appreciation as a way to celebrate, not to manipulate.

When we use NVC to express appreciation, it is purely to celebrate, not to get something in return. Our sole intention is to celebrate the way our lives have been enriched by others.

The Three Components Of Appreciation

NVC clearly distinguishes three components in the expression of appreciation:

1) the actions that have contributed to our well-being;
2) the particular needs of ours that have been fulfilled; and
3) the pleasureful feelings engendered by the fulfillment of those needs.

The sequence of these ingredients may vary; sometimes all three can be conveyed by a smile or a simple "Thank you." However, if

Saying "thank you" in NVC: "This is what you did; this is what I feel; this is the need of mine that was met."

we want to ensure that our appreciation has been fully received, it is valuable to develop the eloquence to express all three components verbally. The following dialogue illustrates how praise may be transformed into an appreciation that embraces all three components.

Participant (approaching me at end of a workshop): Marshall, you're brilliant!

MBR: I'm not able to get as much out of your appreciation as I would like.

Participant: Why, what do you mean?

MBR: In my lifetime I've been called a multitude of names, yet I can't recall seriously learning anything by being told what I am. I'd like to learn from your appreciation and enjoy it, but I would need more information.

Participant: Like what?

MBR: First, I'd like to know what I said or did that made life more wonderful for you.

Participant: Well, you're so intelligent.

MBR: I'm afraid you've just given me another judgment that still leaves me wondering what I did that made life more wonderful for you.

　　The participant thinks for a while, but then she points to notes she had taken during the workshop, "Look at these two places. It was these two things you said."

MBR: Ah, so it's my saying those two things that you appreciate.

Participant: Yes.

MBR: Next, I'd like to know how you feel in conjunction to my having said those two things.

Participant: Hopeful and relieved.

MBR: And now I'd like to know what needs of yours were fulfilled by my saying those two things.

Participant: I have this 18-year-old son whom I haven't been able to communicate with. I'd been desperately searching for some direction that might help me to relate with him in a more loving manner, and those two things you said provide the direction I was looking for.

Hearing all three pieces of information—what I did, how she felt, and what needs of hers were fulfilled—I could then celebrate the appreciation with her. Had she initially expressed her appreciation in NVC, it might have sounded like this: "Marshall, when you said these two things [showing me her notes], I felt very hopeful and relieved, because I've been searching for a way to make a connection with my son, and these gave me the direction I was looking for."

Receiving Appreciation

Many of us do not receive appreciation gracefully. We fret over whether we deserve it. We worry about what's being expected of us—especially if we have teachers or managers who use appreciation as a means to spur productivity. Or we're nervous about living up to the appreciation. Accustomed to a culture where buying, earning, and deserving are the standard modes of interchange, we are often uncomfortable with simple giving and receiving.

NVC encourages us to receive appreciation with the same quality of empathy we express when listening to other messages. We hear what we have done that has contributed to others' well-being; we hear their feelings and the needs that were fulfilled. We take into our hearts the joyous reality that we can each enhance the quality of others' lives.

I was taught to receive appreciation with grace by my friend, Nafez Assailey. He was a member of a Palestinian team whom I had invited to Switzerland for training in NVC at a time when security precautions made training of mixed groups of Palestinians and Israelis impossible in either of their own countries. At the end of the workshop, Nafez came up to me. "This training will be very valuable for us in working for peace in our country," he acknowledged. "I would like to thank you in a way that we Sufi Muslims do when we want to express special appreciation for something." Locking his thumb onto mine, he looked me in the eye and said, "I kiss the God in you that allows you to give us what you did." He then kissed my hand.

Nafez's expression of gratitude showed me a different way to receive appreciation. Usually it is received from one of two polar positions. At one end is egotism: believing ourselves to be

> **Receive appreciation without feelings of superiority or false humility.**

superior because we've been appreciated. At the other extreme is false humility, denying the importance of the appreciation by shrugging it off: "Oh, it was nothing." Nafez showed me that I could receive appreciation joyfully, in the awareness that God has given everyone the power to enrich the lives of others. If I am aware that it is this power of God working through me that gives me the power to enrich life for others, then I may avoid both the ego trap and the false humility.

Golda Meir, when she was the Israeli prime minister, once chided one of her ministers: "Don't be so humble, you're not that great." The following lines, attributed to contemporary writer Marianne Williamson, serve as another reminder for me to avoid the pitfall of false humility:

> Our deepest fear is not that we are inadequate. Our deepest fear is that we are powerful beyond measure.
>
> It is our light, not our darkness, that frightens us. You are a child of God. Your playing small doesn't serve the world.
>
> There's nothing enlightened about shrinking so that other people won't feel insecure around you.
>
> We were born to make manifest the glory of God that is within us. It's not just in some of us, it is in everyone.
>
> And as we let our own light shine, we unconsciously give other people permission to do the same.
>
> As we are liberated from our fear, our presence automatically liberates others.

The Hunger For Appreciation

Paradoxically, despite our unease in receiving appreciation, most of us yearn to be genuinely recognized and appreciated. During a surprise party for me, a 12-year-old friend of mine suggested a party game to help introduce the guests to each other. We were to write down a question, drop it in a box, and then take turns, each person drawing out a question and responding to it out loud.

Having recently consulted with various social service agencies and industrial organizations, I was feeling struck by how often people expressed a hunger for appreciation on the job. "No matter how hard you work," they would sigh, "you never hear a good word from anyone. But make one mistake and there's always someone jumping all over you." So for the game, I wrote the question, "What appreciation might someone give you that would leave you jumping for joy?"

A woman drew that question out of the box, read it, and started to cry. As director of a shelter for battered women, she would put considerable energy each month into creating a schedule to please as many people as possible. Yet each time the schedule was presented, at least a couple of individuals would complain. She couldn't remember ever receiving appreciation for her efforts to design a fair schedule. All this had flashed through her mind as she read my question, and the hunger for appreciation brought tears to her eyes.

Upon hearing the woman's story, another friend of mine said that he, too, would like to answer the question. Everyone else then requested a turn; as they responded to the question, several people wept.

While the craving for appreciation—as opposed to manipulative "strokes"—is particularly evident in the workplace, it affects family life as well. One evening when I pointed out his failure to perform a house chore, my son Brett retorted, "Dad, are you aware how often you bring up what's gone wrong but almost never bring up what's gone right?" His observation

> We tend to notice what's wrong rather than what's right.

stayed with me. I realized how I was continually searching for improvements, while barely stopping to celebrate things that were going well. I had just completed a workshop with over a hundred participants, all of whom had evaluated it very highly, with the exception of one person. However, what lingered in my mind was that one person's dissatisfaction.

That evening I wrote a song that began,
"If I'm ninety eight percent perfect
in anything I do,
it's the two percent I've messed up
I'll remember when I'm through."

It occurred to me that I had a choice to adopt instead the outlook of a teacher I knew. One of her students, having neglected to study for an exam, had resigned himself to turning in a blank piece of paper with his name at the top.. He was surprised when she later returned the test to him with a grade of 14%. "What did I get 14% for?" he asked incredulously. "Neatness," she replied. Ever since my son Brett's "wake-up call," I've tried to be more aware of what others around me are doing that enriches my life and to hone my skills in expressing this appreciation.

Overcoming The Reluctance To Express Appreciation

I was deeply touched by a passage in John Powell's book, *The Secret of Staying in Love*, in which he describes his sadness over having been unable, during his father's lifetime, to express the appreciation he felt for him. How grievous it seemed to me to miss the chance of appreciating the people who have been the greatest positive influences in our lives!

Immediately an uncle of mine, Julius Fox, came to mind. When I was a boy, he came daily to offer nursing care to my grandmother, who was totally paralyzed. While he cared for my grandmother, he always had a warm and loving smile on his face. No matter how unpleasant the task may have appeared to my boyish eyes, he treated her as if she were doing him the greatest favor in the world by letting him care for her. This provided a wonderful model of masculine strength for me—one that I've often called upon in the years since.

I realized that I had never expressed my appreciation for my uncle, who himself was now ill and near death. I considered doing so, but sensed my own resistance: "I'm sure he already knows how much he means to me, I don't need to express it out loud; besides, it might embarrass him if I put it into words." As soon as these thoughts entered my head, I already knew they weren't true. Too often I had assumed that others knew the intensity of my appreciation for them, only to discover otherwise. And even when people were embarrassed, they still wanted to hear appreciation verbalized.

Still hesitant, I told myself that words couldn't do justice to the depths of what I wished to communicate. I quickly saw through that one, though: yes, words may be poor vehicles in conveying our heartfelt realities, but as I have learned, "Anything that is worth doing is worth doing poorly!"

As it happened, I soon found myself seated next to Uncle Julius at a family gathering and the words simply flowed out of me. He took them in joyfully, without embarrassment. Brimming over with feelings from the evening, I went home, composed a poem and sent it to him. I was later told that, each day until he died three weeks later, my uncle had asked that the poem be read to him.

Summary

Conventional compliments often take the form of judgments, however positive, and are sometimes offered to manipulate the behavior of others. NVC encourages the expression of appreciation solely for celebration. We state (1) the action that has contributed to our well-being, (2) the particular need of ours that has been fulfilled, and (3) the feeling of pleasure engendered as a result.

When we receive appreciation expressed in this way, we can do so without any feeling of superiority or false humility by celebrating along with the person who is offering the appreciation.

Epilogue

I once asked my uncle Julius how he had developed such a remarkable capacity to give compassionately. He seemed honored by my question, which he pondered before replying, "I've been blessed with good teachers." When I asked who these were, he recalled, "Your grandmother was the best teacher I had. You lived with her when she was already ill, so you didn't know what she was really like. For example, did your mother ever tell you about the time during the Depression when she brought a tailor and his wife and two children to live with her for three years, after he lost his house and business?" I remembered the story well. It had left a deep impression when my mother first told it to me because I could never figure out where Grandmother had found space for the tailor's family when she was raising nine children of her own in a modest-sized house!

Uncle Julius recollected my grandmother's compassion in a few more anecdotes, all of which I had heard as a child. Then he asked, "Surely your mother told you about Jesus."

"About who?"

"Jesus."

"No, she never told me about Jesus."

The story about Jesus was the final precious gift I received from my uncle before he died. It's a true story of a time when a man came to my grandmother's back door asking for some food. This wasn't unusual. Although Grandmother was very poor, the entire neighborhood knew that she would feed anyone who showed up at her door. The man had a beard and wild scraggly black hair; his clothes were ragged and he wore a cross around his neck fashioned out of branches tied with rope. My grandmother invited him into her kitchen for some food, and while he was eating she asked his name.

"My name is Jesus," he replied.

"Do you have a last name?" she inquired.

"I am Jesus the Lord." (My grandmother's English wasn't too good. Another uncle, Isidor, later told me he had come into the kitchen while the man was still eating and Grandmother had introduced the stranger as "Mr. Thelord.")

As he continued to eat, my grandmother asked where he lived.

"I don't have a home."

"Well, where are you going to stay tonight? It's cold."

"I don't know."

"Would you like to stay here?" she offered.

He stayed seven years.

When it came to communicating nonviolently, my grandmother was a natural. She didn't think of what this man "was." If she did, she probably would have judged him as crazy and gotten rid of him. No, she thought in terms of what people feel and what they need. If they're hungry, feed them. If they're without a roof over their head, give them a place to sleep.

My grandmother loved to dance, and my mother remembers her saying often, "Never walk when you can dance." And thus I end this book on a language of compassion with a song about my grandmother, who spoke and lived the language of Nonviolent Communication.

> *One day a man named Jesus*
> *came around to my grandmother's door.*
> *He asked for a little food,*
> *she gave him more.*
>
> *He said he was Jesus the Lord;*
> *she didn't check him out with Rome.*
> *He stayed for several years,*
> *as did many without a home.*
>
> *It was in her Jewish way,*
> *she taught me what Jesus had to say.*
> *In that precious way,*
> *she taught me what Jesus had to say.*

And that's: "Feed the hungry, heal the sick,
then take a rest.
Never walk when you can dance;
make your home a cozy nest."

It was in her Jewish way,
she taught me what Jesus had to say.
In her precious way,
she taught me what Jesus had to say.

www.NonviolentCommunication.com

Please visit the publisher's website for more information about Nonviolent Communication, the author, links to regional NVC related websites, and reference materials relating to the specific application of Nonviolent Communication in different situations.

We are committed to enhancing our website with new reference material on an ongoing basis so please visit frequently and recommend our website to your friends and associates so they too can learn about Nonviolent Communication. Thank you.

Bibliography

Alinsky, Saul D. Rules for Radicals: *A Practical Primer for Realistic Radicals.* New York: Random House, 1971.

Becker, Ernest. *The Birth and Death of Meaning.* New York: Free Press, 1971.

Becker, Ernest. *The Revolution in Psychiatry: The New Understanding Of Man.* New York: Free Press, 1964.

Benedict, Ruth. "Synergy-Patterns of the Good Culture." *Psychology Today.* June 1970.

Boserup, Anders and Mack, Andrew. *War Without Weapons: Non-Violence in National Defense.* New York: Schocken, 1975.

Bowles, Samuel and Gintis, Herbert. *Schooling in Capitalist America: Educational Reform and the Contradictions of Economic Life.* New York: Basic Books, 1976.

Buber, Martin. *I and Thou.* New York: Scribner, 1958.

Craig, James and Marguerite. *Synergic Power.* Berkeley, CA: Proactive Press, 1974.

Dass, Ram. *The Only Dance There Is.* Harper & Row, 1974.

Dass, Ram and Bush, Mirabai. *Compassion in Action: Setting Out on the Path of Service.* New York: Bell Tower, 1992.

Dass, Ram and Gorman, Paul. *How Can I Help?: Stories and Reflections on Service.* New York: Knopf, 1985.

Domhoff, William G. *The Higher Circles: The Governing Class in America.* New York: Vintage Books, 1971.

Ellis, Albert. *A Guide to Rational Living.* Wilshire Book Co., 1961.

Freire, Paulo. *Pedagogy of the Oppressed.* Herder and Herder, 1971.

Fromm, Erich. *Escape from Freedom.* Holt, Rinehart & Winston, 1941.

Fromm, Erich. *The Art of Loving.* Harper & Row, 1956.

Gardner, Herb, "A Thousand Clowns" from *The Collected Plays*, Applause Books, 2000

Gendlin, Eugene. *Focusing.* Living Skills Media Center, Portland, OR, 1978.

Glenn, Michael and Kunnes, Richard. *Repression or Revolution.* Harper and Row, 1973.

Greenburg, Dan and Jacobs, Marcia. *How to Make Yourself Miserable.* New York: Vintage Books, 1987.

Harvey, O.J. *Conceptual Systems and Personality Organization.* Harper & Row, 1961.

Hillesum, Etty. *A Diary.* Jonathan Cape, 1983

Holt, John. *How Children Fail.* New York: Pitman, 1964.

Humphreys, Christmas. *The Way of Action.* Penguin Books, 1960.

Irwin, Robert. *Nonviolent Social Defense.* Harper & Row, 1962.

Johnson, Wendell. *Living with Change.* New York: Harper and Row, 1972.

Katz, Michael. *Class, Bureaucracy and the Schools.* Preager text Publishers, 2nd ed., 1975.

Katz, Michael. *School Reform: Past and Present.* Boston, Little, Brown & Co., 1971.

Kaufmann, Walter. *Without Guilt and Justice.* New York: P.H. Wyden, 1973.

Keen, Sam. *To a Dancing God.* New York: Harper and Row, 1970.

Keen, Sam. *Hymns To An Unknown God: Awakening The Spirit In Everyday Life.* New York: Bantam Books, 1994.

Kelly, George A. *The Psychology of Personal Constructs.* Volumes 1 & 2. New York: Norton, 1955.

Kornfield, Jack. *A Path with Heart: A Guide Through the Perils and Promises of Spiritual Life.* New York: Bantam Books, 1993.

Kozol, Jonathan. *The Night is Dark and I Am Far from Home.* Boston: Houghton-Mifflin Co., 1975.

Kurtz, Ernest, and Ketcham, Katherine. *The Spirituality of Imperfection: Modern Wisdom from Classic Stories.* New York: Bantam Books, 1992.

Lyons, Gracie. *Constructive Criticism.* Oakland, CA: IRT Press, 1977.

Mager, Robert. *Preparing Instructional Objectives.* Fearon Pub., 1962.

Maslow, Abraham. *Eupsychian Management.* Dorsey Press, 1965.

Maslow, Abraham. *Toward a Psychology of Being.* Princeton, NJ: Van Nostrand, 1962.

McLaughlin, Corinne and Davidson, Gordon. *Spiritual Politics: Changing the World from the Inside Out.* New York: Ballantine Books, 1994.

Milgram, Stanley. *Obedience to Authority.* New York: Harper and Row, 1974.

Postman, Neil and Weingartner, Charles. *Teaching as a Subversive Activity.* Delacorte, 1969.

Postman, Neil and Weingartner, Charles. *The Soft Revolution: A Student Handbook for Turning Schools Around.* New York: Delta, 1971.

Powell, John. *The Secret of Staying in Love.* Niles, IL: Argus, 1974.

Powell, John. *Why Am I Afraid to Tell You Who I Am?* Niles, IL: Argus, 1976.

Putney, Snell. *The Conquest of Society.* Belmont, CA: Wadsworth, 1972.

Robben, John. *Coming to My Senses.* New York: Thomas Crowell, 1973.

Rogers, Carl. *Freedom to Learn.* Charles E. Merrill, 1969.

Rogers, Carl. *On Personal Power.* New York: Delacorte, 1977.

Rogers, Carl. "Some Elements of Effective Interpersonal Communication." Mimeographed paper from speech given at California Institute of Technology, Pasadena, CA, Nov. 9, 1964.

Rosenberg, Marshall. *Mutual Education: Toward Autonomy and Interdependence.* Seattle: Special Child Publications, 1972.

Ryan, William. *Blaming the Victim.* New York: Vintage Books, 1971.

Scheff, Thomas. *Labeling Madness.* Englewood Cliffs, NJ: Prentice-Hall, 1975.

Schmookler, Andrew Bard. *Out of Weakness: Healing the Wounds that Drive Us to War.* New York: Bantam Books, 1988.

Sharp, Gene. *Social Power and Political Freedom.* Boston: Porter Sargent, 1980.

Steiner, Claude. *Scripts People Live.* Grove Press, 1974.

Szasz, Thomas. *Ideology and Insanity.* New York: Doubleday, 1970.

Tagore, Rabindranath. *Sadhana: The Realization of Life.* Tucson: Omen Press, 1972.

Index

A

accountability
  for anger, 141–42
  speech patterns that mask, 49–52
  see also responsibility
action language, positive, 69
action requests, 67
advice vs. empathy, 92–93, 97–98
age role as behavior excuse, 20
aggression, in response to blame and judgment, 148
  see also judgments; violence
Amtssprache, 19, 140
analyses of others, as expression of values and needs, 16, 52–54, 153, 174
  see also judgments
anger
  and blame, 50, 141–43, 174–75
  four steps to expressing, 148
  NVC in Action dialogue, 154–59
  stimulus vs. cause, 141–43, 145–48
  unfulfilled needs at core of, 144–45
appreciation, 75, 185–92
approval, as motivator, 138
Arendt, Hannah, 19
Assailey, Nafez, 188–89
attention, focusing on NVC components, 3–4, 6

B

Babble-on-ians, 121–22

"bad"/"good" labels, 17–18, 23, 130, 132
Bebermeyer, Ruth (songs), xii, 5, 27–28, 67
Becker, Ernest, 172
behavior excuses, 19–20
beliefs
  as basis of value judgments, 17
  about ethnic and racial groups, 143–46
  about gender roles, 55–57
Bernanos, George, 21–22
blame
  anger as, 50, 141–43, 174–75
  as punishment, 163
  as response to negative messages, 94
  self-, 49–50, 130–31
  see also negative messages
boring conversations, 121–23
Bryson, Kelly, 121–22
Buber, Martin, 91–92, 175–76
Buechner, Frederick, 25

C

Campbell, Joseph, 100
cause vs. stimulus of feelings, 49, 141–43, 145–48
Chardin, Teilhard de, 170
choices, 19–21, 130–31, 136–40
Chuang-Tzu, 91
clinical language vs. NVC, 175–79
"cognitively arrested alternatives", 172
comparisons as judgment, 19

Notes

Some Basic Feelings We All Have

Feelings when needs "are" fulfilled

- Amazed
- Confident
- Energetic
- Glad
- Inspired
- Joyous
- Optimistic
- Relieved
- Surprised
- Touched
- Comfortable
- Eager
- Fulfilled
- Hopeful
- Intrigued
- Moved
- Proud
- Stimulated
- Thankful
- Trustful

Feelings when needs "are not" fulfilled

- Angry
- Confused
- Disappointed
- Distressed
- Frustrated
- Hopeless
- Irritated
- Nervous
- Puzzled
- Sad
- Annoyed
- Concerned
- Discouraged
- Embarrassed
- Helpless
- Impatient
- Lonely
- Overwhelmed
- Reluctant
- Uncomfortable

Some Basic Needs We All Have

Autonomy
- Choosing dreams/goals/values
- Choosing plans for fulfilling one's dreams, goals, values

Celebration
- Celebrate the creation of life and dreams fulfilled
- Celebrate losses: loved ones, dreams, etc. (mourning)

Integrity
- Authenticity • Creativity
- Meaning • Self-worth

Interdependence
- Acceptance • Appreciation
- Closeness • Community
- Consideration
- Contribute to the enrichment of life
- Emotional Safety • Empathy

Physical Nurturance
- Air • Food
- Movement, exercise
- Protection from life-threatening forms of life: viruses, bacteria, insects, predatory animals
- Rest • Sexual expression
- Shelter • Touch • Water

Play
- Fun • Laughter

Spiritual Communion
- Beauty • Harmony
- Inspiration • Order • Peace

- Honesty (the empowering honesty that enables us to learn from our limitations)
- Love • Reassurance
- Respect • Support
- Trust • Understanding

2428 Foothill Blvd., Suite E, La Crescenta, CA 91214
Tel: (818) 957-9393 • Fax: (818) 957-1424
Email: cnvc@cnvc.org • Website: www.cnvc.org

The **Center for Nonviolent Communication** is a global organization whose vision is a world where everyone's needs are met peacefully. Our mission is to contribute to this vision by facilitating the creation of life-enriching systems within ourselves, inter-personally, and within organizations. We do this by living and teaching the process of Nonviolent Communication^{SM} (NVC), which strengthens people's ability to compassionately connect with themselves and one another, share resources, and resolve conflicts peacefully.

CNVC is dedicated to fostering a compassionate response to people by honoring our universally shared needs for autonomy, celebration, integrity, interdependence, physical nurturance, play, and spiritual communion. We are committed to functioning, at every level of our organization and in all of our interactions, in harmony with the process we teach, operating by consensus, using NVC to resolve conflicts, and providing NVC training for our staff. We often work collaboratively with other organizations for a peaceful, just and ecologically balanced world.

Purpose, Mission, History, and Projects

What NVC Is—It is a powerful process for inspiring compassionate connection and action. It provides a framework and set of skills to address human problems, from the most intimate relationships to global political conflicts. NVC can help prevent conflicts as well as peacefully resolve them. NVC helps us to focus on the feelings and needs we all have, instead of thinking and speaking in terms of dehumanizing labels or other habitual patterns—which are easily heard as demanding and antagonistic, and which contribute to violence towards ourselves, others, and the world around us. NVC empowers people to engage in a creative dialogue in order to construct their own fully satisfactory solutions.

Where NVC Came From—Marshall B. Rosenberg first developed the NVC process in 1963 and he has been continuously refining it ever since. Rosenberg learned about violence at an early age and developed a strong desire to understand what contributed to people being violent to one another, and to explore what kind of language, thought, and communication could provide peaceful alternatives to the violence he encountered. His interest led to graduate school, where he earned a Ph.D. in clinical psychology. He first used NVC to support communities working to peacefully integrate schools and other public institutions during the 1960's. His work on these projects brought Dr. Rosenberg into contact with people in various U.S. cities who wanted to bring his training to a broad base of people in their communities. To meet this need and to more effectively spread the process of NVC, in 1984 he founded the Center for Nonviolent Communication (CNVC) and has since created many materials, including two trade edition books: *Nonviolent Communication: A Language of Life*, 2nd Edition, and *Life-Enriching Education.*

For many years the Center for Nonviolent Communication has been contributing to a vast social transformation in thinking, speaking and acting—showing people how to connect in ways that inspire compassionate results. Training in NVC is now offered throughout the world by Dr. Rosenberg and a team of more than 100 certified trainers, and is supported by hundreds of committed volunteers who help organize workshops, participate in practice groups, and coordinate team building. The training is helping prevent and resolve conflicts in schools, businesses, health care centers, prisons, community groups and families. Marshall Rosenberg and his associates have introduced NVC in war torn areas such as Sierra Leone, Sri Lanka, Rwanda, Burundi, Bosnia and Serbia, Colombia and the Middle East.

We are now seeking funds to support projects in including North America, Latin America, South America, Europe, Africa, South Asia, Brazil, and the Middle East. Foundation grants have helped launch CNVC innovative learning projects to create resources for educators, and projects that focus on parenting, social change, and prison work in various geographical regions of the world. We are working in synergy with other organizations whose missions are aligned with ours. Please visit the CNVC website for information about these projects, regional websites, and for other resources available for learning NVC. Your contribution in support of these efforts will be greatly appreciated.

A list of CNVC certified trainers and contact information for them may be found on the Center's website. This list is updated monthly. The website also includes information about CNVC sponsored trainings and links to affiliated regional websites. CNVC invites you to consider bringing NVC training to your business, school, church, or community group. For current information about trainings scheduled in your area, or if you would like to organize NVC trainings, be on the CNVC mailing list or support our efforts to create a more peaceful world, please contact CNVC.

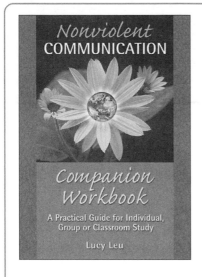

Nonviolent Communication℠ Companion Workbook

by Lucy Leu

ISBN: 1-892005-04-2
Trade Paper 7x10 • Price: $19.95 US
Distributed by IPG: 800-888-4741

*Create your life, your
relationships, and your world
in harmony with your values.*

It's time to put Nonviolent Communication into practice, and this workbook will help you do it. Supporting you through each chapter of Rosenberg's book, this workbook contains refreshing and empowering ideas for: dealing with anger, resolving conflict, improving internal dialogue, and relating more compassionately with others.

• For **INDIVIDUALS**, this workbook provides you with activities and ideas for employing the liberating principles of NVC in your daily life.

• For **GROUP PRACTICE**, this workbook offers guidance for getting started, curriculum, and activities for each chapter.

• For **TEACHERS**, this workbook serves as the basis for developing your own courses, or to augment an existing curriculum.

LUCY LEU is the former Board President of the Center for Nonviolent Communication, and editor of the best selling *Nonviolent Communication: A Language of Life*. Currently she heads the Freedom Project, bringing NVC training to prison inmates to contribute to their reintegration into society. For information about the Freedom Project email: freedom_project@hotmail.com

Available from CNVC, all major bookstores and Amazon.com
Distributed by IPG: 800-888-4741

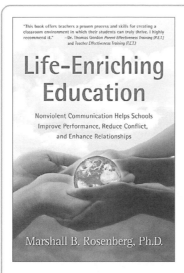

Life-Enriching Education

by Marshall B. Rosenberg, Ph.D.

ISBN: 1-892005-05-0
Trade Paper 6x9 • Price: $12.95 US
Distributed by IPG: 800-888-4741

*When Students Love to Learn
and Teachers Love to Teach . . .*

Today many schools struggle with low achievement, disrespect among students and teachers, and safety issues as their primary concerns. Students and their families are unhappy, teachers and administrators are frustrated, and everyone can't wait for the weekend.

What's needed is a new approach to education, one that serves the lives of everyone in the learning community. Marshall Rosenberg realizes this vision in Life-Enriching Education. You'll discover an approach to education based on mutually respectful relationships between students, teachers, administrators, and parents.

You'll learn practical skills that show you how to:

- Increase student interest, achievement, and retention
- Create a safe and supportive learning and working atmosphere
- Cultivate emotional intelligence, respect, and compassion
- Resolve conflicts and prevent or de-escalate violence
- Re-discover the joy of teaching motivated students

"This book offers teachers a proven process, and skills for creating a classroom environment in which their students can truly thrive. I highly recommend it."

—Dr. Thomas Gordon Author, *Parent Effectiveness Training* (P.E.T.) and *Teacher Effectiveness Training* (T.E.T.)

Available from CNVC, all major bookstores and Amazon.com
Distributed by IPG: 800-888-4741

NVC Booklets from PuddleDancer Press

We Can Work It Out $6
Resolving Conflicts Peacefully and Powerfully   (6x9, 32 pages)
by Marshall B. Rosenberg, Ph.D. • Practical suggestions for
fostering caring, genuine cooperation, and satisfying resolutions in
even the most difficult situations.

Teaching Children Compassionately $8
How Students and Teachers Can Succeed with Mutual   (6x9, 48 pages)
Understanding • by Marshall B. Rosenberg, Ph.D.
Skills for creating a successful classroom—from a keynote address and
workshop given to a national conference of Montessori educators.

What's Making You Angry? $6
10 Steps to Transforming Anger So Everyone Wins   (6x9, 32 pages)
by Shari Klein and Neill Gibson • A step-by-step guide to
re-focus your attention when you're angry, and create outcomes that
are satisfying for everyone.

The Heart of Social Change $8
How to Make a Difference in Your World   (6x9, 48 pages)
by Marshall B. Rosenberg, Ph.D. • Marshall offers an insightful
perspective on effective social change, and how-to examples.

Parenting From Your Heart $8
Sharing the Gifts of Compassion, Connection, and Choice   (6x9, 48 pages)
by Inbal Kashtan • Addresses the challenges of parenting with real-
world solutions for creating family relationships that meet everyone's needs.

Getting Past the Pain Between Us $8
Healing and Reconciliation Without Compromise   (6x9, 48 pages)
by Marshall B. Rosenberg, Ph.D. • Learn the healing power of
listening and speaking from the heart. Skills for resolving conflicts,
healing old hurts, and reconciling strained relationships.

Available from CNVC, order from www.CNVC.org or call 800-255-7696
For more information about these booklets visit
www.NonviolentCommunication.com

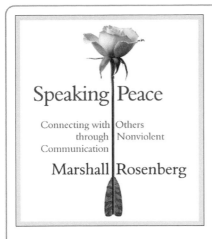

NONVIOLENT COMMUNICATION MATERIALS

Available from CNVC at www.CNVC.org or call 800-255-7696

The Compassionate Classroom $18
Relationship Based Teaching and Learning   (7.5x9, 187 pages)
by Sura Hart and Victoria Kindle Hodson, M.A. • This new book provides
an overview of the NVC process and its relationship to successful teaching and learning,
and specific examples of how NVC can be used in elementary school classrooms includes
playful exercises, lesson plans, and skill-building activities and games.

Raising Children Compassionately $6
Parenting the Nonviolent Communication Way   (24 pages)
by Marshall B. Rosenberg, Ph.D. • This booklet, filled with insights and stories,
will prove invaluable for parents, teachers and others who want to nurture children and
also themselves.

The Giraffe Classroom $18
by Nancy Sokol Green • Humorous, creative, and   (8.5x11, spiral bound, 122 pages)
thought provoking activities. Ideal for teachers, parents, and anyone who wants to use
concrete exercises to learn the process of NVC.

The Mayor of Jackal Heights $10
by Rita Herzog and Kathy Smith • A boy mayor   (8.5x11, spiral bound, 122 pages)
begins to learn how to tame his town full of jackals with the help of his wise friend,
Giraffe. A beautifully illustrated story for children of all ages.

A Model for Nonviolent Communication $8
by Marshall B. Rosenberg • A handbook describing the basics   (5.5x8.5, 56 pages)
of Nonviolent Communication, including exercises to help readers check their
understanding of the process. Updated, expanded, and revised.

Duck Tales and Jackal Taming Hints $4
by Marshall B. Rosenberg, Ph.D. • A whimsical tale about skills   (7x9, 28 pages)
needed to understand human beings, even when their communication makes them
sound like deranged jackals.

Communication Basics $4
An Overview of Nonviolent Communication   (24 pages)
by Rachelle Lamb • This new booklet provides a clear, concise, and handy summary
of what one might learn in an introductory training in Nonviolent Communication.

The Spiritual Basis of Nonviolent Communication $2
A Question and Answer Session with   (8.5x11, 8 pages)
Marshall Rosenberg, Ph.D. • Las Bases Espirituales De La Communicacion No
Violenta—Spanish language version available at same price.

Audiotapes, CDs, and Videotapes

Introduction To A Model for Nonviolent Communication $10
by Marshall B. Rosenberg, Ph.D. • Marshall Rosenberg introduces   (Audio, 90 min.)
a model for Nonviolent Communication through discussion, stories, and music.